GOD

A PATH TO RIGHTEOUSNESS

by

Khadeem Jibreel Thomas

Edited by Tottianna Davis

Copyright © 2019 by Khadeem J Thomas

All rights reserved. This book or any portion thereof may not be reproduced or used in any manner whatsoever without the express written permission of the publisher except for the use of brief quotations in a book review or scholarly journal.

First Printing: 2019

ISBN 978-1-387-69603-1

www.weRICHeous.com

Moments

Water

Duality

Trinity

Manifestation

Healing

Language

Completion

4ever

A.R.T.

Truth

L's

Water

In the beginning God created the heaven and the earth. And the earth was without form, and void; and darkness was upon the face of the deep. And the Spirit of God moved upon the face of the waters. And God said, Let there be light: and there was light. (Genesis 1:1-3)

The *Word* which started it *all* was simply a Vibration. After <u>The Awakening</u>, begin to discover subtle truths about Life here on Earth such as: everything in existence is the product of *energy*, *numbers* are a work of *art*, and we are the *cure* for the dis-ease we created.

Before the *Word*, there existed only water and darkness, imagine that. Many may not talk about earth before light but there, we receive much of our revelation. We did not spontaneously come to be, contrary the narrative we have been told. Today, in the Age of Knowing, learn what life is about.

Although water is the first element Life experiences, Energy is best described in the four fundamental elements: Fire, Water, Earth, and Air. For starters, *fire* is combustion, bright light, and warmth, but fire is also the emotional body we house. Our inner light is fire, our passion, anger, gumption, etc. all derived from fire.

The fire in me comes from my Dad, because anything he wants, he goes and works for it. And he remains cool in the midst of work. I love my Dad and while his passion for what he wants is marveled at, I pray he sees beyond materials becoming more focused on intangibles as they hold the *true* value. Materials can be replaced at a moment's notice, but ideals such as: love, time, and service are only fulfilled while opportunities last. Fire is everlasting while sparks fade.

Water, a representation of our Mind, manifests ideas into matter. The fluidity of my Mind is due to the influence of my older brother. As he instilled in me at an early age to think for myself, my Mind naturally grew stronger. He continuously challenges my perspective, offering more to be considered.

The Mind is a river or a pond, tossing in a pebble are thoughts, creating reality. I dream to be water, adapting to a changing lifestyle with my brothers doing the same, maintaining consistent communication throughout our journeys. A symbol of purity water is, as it cleanses naturally.

Earth, the physical body, the planet we consume, deserves our care. As of today, change is eminent because humans determine the fate of all Life. Also, the Body represents health so we must be mindful of our condition. Here in the material realm, change is not immediate, but it is where it's noticed.

My consciousness in physicality is rooted in my relationship with my Uncle. A former police officer, real estate agent, yoga instructor, etc., he is aware of what he consumes, doing what's necessary to remain healthy and active. Also note, that no-thing is permanent in the body, and with enough conscious effort you can change anything. Further, we must remember to not only consume earth, but to aid Her in production as we are producers as well.

Lastly is *air* and we do not know the origins, but we know it's experienced. Although we may be able to detect direction, we have no proof of initiation. As with the Spirit we do not control when He moves, but we ought to move in conjunction to have success. And my step dad exemplifies how to move spiritually in the Earth thus, my teacher in spirituality.

On his spiritual journey, he has been tested on numerous occasions never wavering in Faith. Specifically, leading our household by example of how to operate in the spiritual realm without questioning God's intentions and simply going as directed. Being observant, I recognize his obedience and discipline to the *Word*, although I wish we were exposed to the multitude of teachings about spirituality versus solely connecting to one resource.

Spirituality is being open and receptive to an array of opportunities, because we never know how our opened doors appear.

My entire life growing up I was influenced by my surroundings, granted, a gifted learner but heavily influenced by my circle. My mother was sure to keep my brother and I in the best areas she could afford. Now more than ever, I recognize how vital my mom was and still is to my development as a human *being*.

As a child not fully understanding what my mom meant by "be careful of those you allow around you", I grasp the concept today. Very gullible, I believed much of what I was told by those I trusted, my older brother and my group of friends.

In those days, I didn't value the opinions of feminine energy as I was being shown to neglect that side. Labeled as cry baby, whining, pee body, any type of ridiculing, only made me tougher. Then, I accepted it because it was coming from my brother who was bigger and stronger, though typically, I'd tell me mom which led to the tattletale name.

A natural follower, I received whatever was given and complained or destroyed something in private. It didn't matter what it was; if I could feel power within, I won, because during everyday life I was not embracing my power. It wasn't until adulthood that I realized why.

The energy I keep around me is always good, although had I become an effective leader earlier, I'd be much better off. Going through years of being a follower led me to embracing being a leader. Known for being adaptive, Khadeem Jibreel Thomas is water because we can be serene or tumultuous. Our state being dependent upon the energy we receive or emit. It's up to us, the people, and our **attitude** during our *choice* of thoughts, words, and actions, to create positive realities.

Learning quickly to refrain from reacting, because there, I possess all the control. If I want someone to leave me be there is a definite method. Participating in the games of other people only leads to continuation, so I elect to stop. I learned a lot during school yet not realizing what I was experiencing in the moment.

Now, I have the words to describe my experience such that it appeals to the masses. It begins with, all life is composed of *energy* and death is included within the life cycle. Those who excel, die and live again; some refer to the cyclical process of dying as Ego-death, being Born-again, or even reinventing themselves.

In my school days, I let the reactive Khadeem die but along with that, I tucked way many of my emotions for an extended period. Ironically, I'd only share some of what I felt with women, then girls, seeing as I claim to not seek their opinions. One thing is for certain, they were good with understanding emotion. There are two sides to me, the smart-aleck, and the sweetheart; guys experienced the sarcasm and the girls I liked, the niceness. My way of expressing the masculine and feminine energy I held within.

As we know, 'energy can neither be created nor destroyed, only transformed', which is the Law of the

Conservation of Energy. Our energy is something that is always with us, only we must learn to manage it, to continuously progress. I've learned that the emotional side of my *being* was never destroyed, it simply transformed into only being expressible to the ladies I wanted.

I impressed guys with my wit and ability to think well on my feet when it came time to roast each other. And impressing girls with my wit first, then the softer side after they have made the cut or honestly once I got enough courage to be open with them. I didn't know then and even today, how to lead conversation with attractive women who know nothing about me. I had a much easier time interacting with those I was familiar with.

All throughout school I was only known by those I had at least one class with, that's how reserved I was. I didn't participate in extracurricular activities, didn't make the basketball team or volleyball team because I lacked the aggression to attract the coaches' attention. Also, because I wasn't very good at it, decent among friends but not enough to represent the school as our elite. Being reserved led to me being overlooked by the masses.

My energy was contingent upon those I surrounded myself with, I kept them smiling with humor and they kept me smiling with humor. Much of my happiness was based on laughter and it was typically directed at others sadly, if only I'd demonstrated more balance. Being reserved didn't make me exempt from karma, as it's something that we all know of but not necessarily the intricacies.

My karma led me to getting beat up in the school bathroom by one of my classmates. He was pants-ed and I laughed with the rest of the class, but I was singled out because I was the easiest victim. Just to get the encounter over with I didn't avoid going to the restroom, instead I went in knowing something would happen.

As soon as I finished urinating, I was being shoved then hit in the side of the face. I quickly went into defense mode and covered my entire face and head because I wasn't going to be hit anymore. He tried to bang my head on the wall, but my arms were the only thing receiving contact. Eventually the school resource officer broke it up and everyone went to class ecstatic. I, however, was upset, not that I lost a fight but because my sensitive nose began bleeding.

Thankful for all the days of elementary and middle school, I am glad they are over. My close-knit friend circle kept me elevated however I did allow too many influences on my *energy*. If I'd known more then, about energy, specifically chakras, I would've been more vocal in change.

Also, I would've respected my fellow peer more and not ridicule them no matter how funny the joke because everyone doesn't have tough skin. I should know firsthand that consistent ridicule leads to improper development because I shut down when I don't appreciate how I am being treated. Acting unbothered to speed up the experience is not the way as growing up isn't fun but acknowledging the growth is imperative for continuation.

You only go as far as your circle and my circle expands every few years. I continuously had to adjust and begin again with a new group of friends, due to my family moving to a new location before each transition into higher education. Allowing my energy to attract whomever to me because I was, and still am introverted. I wouldn't pursue any friendships, they always happened organically. Naturally if your energy is welcoming the right things find you, granted you are living righteous.

My mom did the best she could with my brother and I, and her best is, for lack of better words, the best. Her lessons kept me to a minimum of very close friends, typically I had at least one close friend at each school I attended. Each of my friends playing a pivotal role in my maturation as a human being and I thank them for their contribution because I am not sure who I'd be without them.

To get better is to embrace the uncomfortable situations, a lesson I am just receiving as an adult from a good friend. I was very limited as a kid but not because of mental aptitude as I knew from my mother that I could do anything I put my mind to. Although I recognized her lesson as truth, it didn't make me pursue ideas to see what I could accomplish, I wasn't inspired.

Moved mostly by fear adopted, I steered clear of any opportunities to make myself look foolish. I'd rather be unknown than known for the wrong thing, like getting beat up. I remember a random girl asking me during breakfast if I was the guy that got beat, and I just said "yeah" and turned back around. I couldn't lie about it so I owned up to it. I didn't fight back because it wasn't my first instinct after being hit but I needed the experience.

The way I was taught to fight I'm not sure what the outcome would've been. My brother advised me not to limit my punch but to punch through someone, and while I viewed it as entertainment in the moment, I had no intention of using my power like that. My heart is too light to intentionally harm someone but in the sense of defense, it is understood.

When I would visualize punching through someone, I didn't want the vision to continue long enough for me to see the result. Leading to me lacking trust in myself, not knowing if I would be one not to stop swinging even after recognizing victory. I saw several perspectives and let's just say it happened the way it did for a reason.

I can't imagine walking the halls of Bear Creek as a preteen knowing what I know now. I'd be a monk;

knowing the impact frequencies have on our daily lives, informing my classmates of the dangers of not utilizing all your senses, or how our energy centers are reflected in our behavior, I would've been ostracized or glorified. Neither of which I wanted at the time.

Who would I have been to tell another kid that they like joking on someone else because they are insecure themselves and need to balance their root chakra? Even me, needing to learn how to stand for myself and to not be afraid of walking alone. Many of my situations would've been avoided yet they are what got me *here,* so I am thankful.

Discovery

To see so much
One can only imagine
what's next
As I wonder what's next
I receive a text
Stop wondering what's next
And go have sex
But that's not what I feel
I feel only what's real
And what's real is still surreal
That I AM
The One

The One who understands
The One who overstands
The One who grasps
The concept of Math
While everyone turns away I never stray
From the challenge to learn
How to walk through fire and never burn
How to swim in an ocean of lies
Ensuring my comrades never die
But that they LIVE
In TRUTH

As it's Truth I spread
I sleep better and better in my bed
Although thoughts constantly run through my head
I wonder
About everything I've read
How it all plays a part
In why everyone perceives me to be so smart
In why I've begun to truly appreciate Art
And to think I've always been this way from the start

I accept who I AM
And what I must do
For You
God

Bridge the gaps
between nations
Between stations
Enlighten the masses
Without making learning feel like classes
Teach them
To reach for Him

Polarity

There's a story about two wolves that I'd like to share, and it goes:

An Old Cherokee told his grandson, "My son, there is a battle between two wolves inside us all. One is evil. It is anger, jealousy, greed, resentment, inferiority, lies and ego. The other is good. It is joy, peace, love, hope, humility, kindness, empathy and truth." The boy thought about it and asked, "Grandfather, which wolf wins?" The old man quietly replied, "The one you feed."

An inspiring tale of the two halves within *one*, reminding us of the choice we must make because we possess a power that we ought to utilize. They go by many names representing different perspectives of the same concept, only we are to recognize the complementary parts of the whole to further understand the hole.

Albeit many refer to the Initial Energy as a male figure, the Higher Power is a phenomenon which supersedes sex, encompassing both masculine and feminine energy. Think of

31

Him/Her as a magnet being who you need in the moment whether a Mother or a Father, either end of the gender spectrum. Think of yourself as the same, a being with two sides Ego and Spirit, so which are you investing energy into?

As a Pisces, I am viewed as polarized once anyone learns of my zodiac sign. Many may know us to be indecisive, but we simply see more than the average person. Our symbol is two fish swimming with each other to form a yin yang symbol. This led me to the realization that balance is a key in unlocking our full potential and utilizing it. Being one to overthink, I've learned that I must embrace my feelings more and make balance a focal point in my life. Tasked with the purpose of understanding, Pisces share traits with all eleven other zodiacs, leading us to a connection with anyone.

Along with being a Pisces, I entered this realm on Moon day, the second day of the week, signifying I have a keen understanding of feminine energy. So, not only do I house feminine energy, but I acknowledge and harness it. Along with that, my middle name is Jibreel, corresponding to Archangel Gabriel who is thought to be female, so feminine energy is a part of me in more than one way.

Archangel Gabriel is the messenger of God sent to deliver urgent messages. Imagine knowing this at 13, instead you don't know much about femininity aside from what women display. There are other titles for the consistent polarity we experience here on Earth, recognizing what we are learning is vital to receiving the *message*.

The duality to humans is that we can be beautiful destructive creatures. We are *light beings* that can be impacted by the negativity of darkness which is just as much of an influence as light. Both of which we have equal access to and because we have the choice of light or dark, we typically go with the one which appears to be more appealing.

The influence of positivity and negativity is in the form of frequency; magnets we are, attracting what we exude. Humans that rely heavily on their natural eyes are easily deceived. For me certainly, I had to grow to see beyond the veil of deception into Truth embracing light.

Since darkness uses the power of deception, we are usually deceived into believing *it* is the better option being that visuals are the easiest to fabricate. As kids, it's easiest to be a visual learner, much tougher to be an auditory learner unless it comes naturally which is also possible. To learn from listening is to process much more and interpret in a new way; seeing what's being said.

One must understand diction then be able to imagine the words personified; everyday I'm working to be a better listener as listening requires the utmost patience. I must live by my words, which are to incorporate the other senses that extend beyond the natural eyes.

Beyond the eyes, we can see that each person is fighting a battle between the Ego and the Spirit. The Ego is of flesh, it's your body along with your bodily urges resulting in your animalistic ways. The Ego typically finds a reason why an idea will not work versus the Higher Self revealing the reasons it will work.

The Higher Self is the Spirit dwelling within you, your personal Energy vat, though it may be tough to accept this Truth when we aren't where we desire to be. I know it can be tough for me to accept that I am where I am because of me and no one else. The accountability I developed was in large part due to me learning more about myself through the aspects surrounding us which determine who we are.

Much of what we see in America is through the lenses of a television or cellphone screen thus we are left influenced with sheer negativity feeding our egos. The television is one of the key issues in America as we do not control what it being displayed.

We may think at moments that we are choosing what we wish to watch but we are choosing from the available options.

Even with some sense of freedom through a cellphone, you're still living your life through an artificial reality. Learn life while experiencing life; to have balance within we must begin to seek positivity but first we must recognize negativity in all its forms.

We need to become our own protection from darkness, negativity, and fear. So, we must understand that which we wish to be shielded from to the point we know how to defend against it. If we choose to listen and obey, God will direct our paths, meaning if we become in tune with our intuition it leads to prosperity.

If we live by the sword, we die by the sword; meaning if we choose to live by violence and negativity that is how we will leave. The energy we deliver is that which we will receive so give good to receive good help on the battlefield.

Reading, well listening to the audio book *Outwitting the Devil* gave me so much more perspective on what negativity and fear are. In the book, the devil named church a close second behind school as tools used to propagate negativity. And it's all out of ignorance, our ignorance to learn just enough to feel smart then we neglect our minds until our dying days.

Well this is just what the devil wants, to control the one thing we need to free ourselves. When you relinquish your ability to operate properly, you become a drifter, allowing another entity to assume position. Even if you use your mind sparingly, you liable to drift so we must be conscious of what's going on in our minds at all times.

As a result, our protection then becomes intangible, as in knowledge on how the devil operates. Which will not only make sense but also align with what you have already received as truth. Conversely, there are things I have been told that I simply did not believe no matter who told me, if I didn't feel it, I don't feel it. So, this new perspective was very refreshing because it oozed authenticity that can be felt. What I learned was once you are a drifter, you aren't as aware if aware at all, during waking moments.

Although you would move through life simply existing, going through the motions, you have the power in your mind to create a balanced paradise. Simply put, one who has mastered their fears is one who's mastered themselves. Mastery of Self begets a master in the Earth, placing a one over the devil. If we are to go biblical, the devil was present on earth before humans, yet we are given dominion here. Since we are the influencers of the earth, we must demonstrate balance if we are to have continued protective success.

Furthermore, our choice remains between the Ego and the Spirit; which will you allow to lead you? The Spirit is your connection to the Source which created Life and the Ego is your lower self. Any energy can govern the Ego if it has enough power and wit while making it feel like you are making your own decisions. Now, the Bible warns of being led with the flesh because your decisions will not fulfill your intent.

Consequently, your body is a product of habits as I'm sure our habits are not the most beneficial to our health. Even so, we must have supreme confidence and assurance that our actions are in line with what needs to happen. We do not solely live for us, but we are the only ones we are required to be.

As a matter of fact, no one can live for us no matter what technology exists. We are always the same being, meaning we always have opportunity. Being that opportunity lasts as long as we are alive, we can honestly do whatever we choose. Know though, that any action you perform will be returned to you because the conductor of energy always receives that which was given.

"Realize the energy you give is what you're manifesting" is a line by Big Sean that resonates with me because it's about everything I'm learning about the law of attraction. Leading me to the realization that we must constantly and consistently grow as *beings* hence that's what evolution is, steady growth.

Additionally, I've learned that balance is the key to evolution, our species' goal no matter who you ask. Since we need more perspective on balance, in China, it's referred to as Yin and Yang. Yin Yang can also be looked at as the polarity within that is also displayed throughout the cosmos. Moreover, we were taught in school about earth's magnetic field, but rarely that humans have this same torus surrounding themselves as well.

Our magnetic energy field is the focus of Polarity Therapy, a healing practice which involves focusing energy on blockages along the flow of *energy*. In fact, this magnetic field can also be thought of as your aura, a personalized field attracting all that you are.

Although this may be tough to accept for some because they do not like their status, we must acknowledge that change is the only constant. Anything and everything is bound to change if we are willing to make the necessary adjustments. Are you willing to master balance to evolve?

To illustrate, there's an individual who mastered the art of magnetism, physical balance, a man by the name of Edward Leedskalnin. Ed was a gentleman small in stature but enormous in terms of his creative ability. It's said that he knew the secrets to how the Ancient Egyptians built the pyramids thus he created Coral Castle in Homestead, Florida, near Miami. Never heard of it huh? Yeah, I'm sure.

It was a shock to me as well, discovering that a place of this magnitude existed without anyone ever mentioning it. Coral Castle was the home of Ed, created out of pure coral limestone, each component weighing tons. Ed created this monument by himself, everything perfectly balanced. Good news is he left plenty of clues as to how the feat was accomplished.

Coral Castle is a remarkable landmark standing as evidence of our true capabilities as humans to create structures that stand the test of time. Using magnetism, Ed built this remarkable haven for himself and humanity, call it a gift. Because the earth has its own magnetic field, it can be used to your advantage if you know how to manage it. Edward knew a thing or two about magnetism and its importance.

His level of expertise in skills to harness the potential energy of earth is what I admire. This is the type of wisdom I am seeking, being able to use what is readily available to create masterpieces. Not only creating art but continuously pushing the culture forward and I mean culture in the sense of humanity. It's time to evolve.

How do you evolve? Master your foundation before you build another block on top. How can you expect to stay up with no infrastructure? Everyone is in a rush to go to the top when they don't have a solid structure holding them up. Learn what you need to be as complete as possible until it all changes; retain everything but remember there's another level of mastery.

After mastery of the basics, you master intermediacy, so let's take it up a notch and learn this *life*. Me personally, I must remain open to the possibilities. The truths I am discovering may be incomplete, but I am simply acknowledging what I see thus far, which is enough to get the ball rolling.

Spirit in one perspective, half of everything you are, is masculine, thus why people refer to God as a male figure. Imagine how spirits moves freely through space and time, also notice how many males typically float between females. Today many men are not in tune with their femininity which becomes the root of their dysfunctional relationships with women. We as men must learn to balance the energy within if we are to ever understand our vital counterparts.

Many men want to be with more than one woman, but women want men to understand the attraction to one. We as men feel we can give to more than one woman, but we can be more focused on what we are receiving versus what we are giving. Be inclusive of your feminine counterpart, all senses of body, embrace the divine feminine.

Balance occurs in the Mind because both masculine and feminine energy are united in the Mind. Not only does this makes the *mind* our gift from God, but also a byproduct of the Body and Spirit. Together, Yang and Yin or femininity and masculinity, meet in the mind through Thoughts and Feelings. It's important to realize, Feelings can be both emotional and physical while Thoughts are mental and emotional.

To better manage the bridge of emotion, one can detach from thoughts and feelings not acting upon any occurrences. In detachment, one learns to distinguish between masculine and feminine energy; thoughts are masculine in nature and feelings are feminine, so we are to understand the purpose for both to live efficiently with a sound mind.

Since *man* came from the ground and with the breath of Spirit was given life, that means from femininity came masculinity. Being created from Earth means that we all come from feminine energy as the physical body is feminine in nature. Although male humans were created first according to the Bible, we all come from the same mother, Earth.

Hence why we say Father God and Mother Earth; recognize though, both are God. Even though God is a term that is meant to encompass all, we rarely see it that way. And while many say they believe, they do not understand what their belief system is. That is to say, think about what you feel and feel what you think to align the two realms.

Learning the magnitude of balance led me to a revelation that there is always a complement available. Let alone, the ancient cultures knew balance was sacred thousands of years ago. The ancient Egyptians, specifically, reached a level of consciousness where they innerstood all aspects of themselves represented by *sacred feminine* and *sacred masculine* principles.

To clarify, sacred feminine and masculine are the purest forms of consciousness recognized throughout the body. For example, the right side of the brain and the left side of the body correspond to the *sacred feminine*. While the right side of the body and the left side of the brain correspond to the *sacred masculine*. After you discover universal keys then you begin to see all of the doors you're able to open.

Watching The Pyramid Code I learned, during the period of Ancient Egyptians, it was a Matriarchal society, one acknowledging balance and harmony with *life*. Matriarchal consciousness is associated with eternity, cycles of time, ritual, magic, altered states, and art. While Patriarchal consciousness is associated with history, linear time, dogma, rationality, waking reality, and science. As you can see we are still feeling the influence of patriarchal consciousness in everything, including the way we learn to how we live.

For instance, we can see the imbalance of masculine energy when anything without rigidity is shunned. Not to mention ideals feminine in nature or represent femininity are shut down because in a patriarchal system, feminine is viewed as weak. Above all, I believe that's why ancient cultures were so advanced, they were more balanced throughout the *spirit*, *mind*, and *body*.

Once upon a time we acknowledged the femininity within and honored it to *be* all we could. Then, we began a phase where we didn't have a clue about ourselves. Even though we learned plenty about irrelevant information deigned to keep our minds carnal, today, we are leaving patriarchy into matriarchy.

The process is underway as more individuals are recognizing that they are an individual meaning they are meant to be different from the one next to them. Both masculine and feminine energies are our source of life which dwell within us in the Mind, the central system. Therefore, the Mind is both masculine and feminine, *thought* and *feeling*, left and right brain, look at these as alternatives.

Balance will always *be*, meaning nature will ensure it remains, as it is a universal law which bounds the cosmos together. Equally important, I believe that is why we have the abundance of blurred lines within sexuality and gender today. Our mental spaces need clarity; along with that, we are being ignorant towards our complementary halves, so they are being personified and naturally balanced.

Since men don't want to embrace their femininity, we have a surplus of men wanting to be women and some turning away from women completely, while embodying feminine qualities. Nature is a *responding* phenomenon, always adjusting accordingly, reacting to the energy received and reciprocating it.

Although it is true that misery loves company, what that statement really says is that, again, energy is transformed or transferred from one host to another. While *light* energy breeds, it is *dark* energy that feeds. As children of God, we mustn't judge who is good/bad or distinguish who is worthy of help. We are to treat everyone with the same likeness while keeping a close eye on those we love just as closely as we watch our enemy.

Seeing as there's duality to everything, seek alternative perspectives. They want us to be caught up in superficial content to distract us while they create their desired reality. Remember, darkness only survives when Light is not around, and dark becomes light when light is present, thus Light is the only thing we need to focus on. Light is at the basis of Life and I have learned that three is the basis for everything, Spirit, Mind, and Body.

Breathe

As I breathe
I feel the need
To get on my knees
And Pray
For us all
Why do what someone else say
When you can pave your own way
So do what you may
And remember to stay safe
As Life continues To win you
Must befriend two
To help you get through

How To Be

What does it mean
To continuously live free
Not to focus on the seams
But to exist or rather *be*
Be all you can be
Because then and only then
Will you begin to see
That in order for you to win
You must accept defeat
To live comfortably
And practice accountability
Which is to live responsibly
Keep in mind that it happens best
When it occurs naturally
I would say the rest
But you know how to treat your guest
Like they deserve your respect
To receive respect you must first give
What you require to live

Simply Think

Is Life truly a mystery
Do we have free will
Or is there a such thing as destiny
How do you feel
About your recipe
Is it all for a meal
That we are taught to kill
We need this key

The Key to Life is among us
Don't expect it to be humongous
It's really just beyond us
It's really cause of Karma
Cause we had the pharma
Yeah we had the meds
Sure we can blame the Feds
For what we're being fed
Because it's to ensure we end up dead

Dying is different
But your experience is contingent
Upon your imprint
From heaven you may still be dismissed
If this miss
You might have a conflict
Which can be dismissed
If you find the switch
Turn on the Light
And do what is Right

Trinity

The power of three. Quick shout out to Garrett Odom for an immaculate debut album and for introducing me to the phrase, The Power of 3. The Trinity is thought of as Father, Son, Holy Spirit, but there are more ways to exemplify three. For instance, Faith, Love, and Discipline are what I have learned the Trinity represents.

Also expressed as Energy, Frequency, and Vibration or Spirit, Mind, and Body, they are all one in the same. Man's way of living becomes toxic if it's done on their own merit rather than in conjunction with The All. Religion is Man's way of living, our way of interpreting the Frequency emitted by the Initial Consciousness.

There are three main religions in the Earth and we, as of 2017, have a population of 7.5 billion with most people having either converted or been born into Judaism,

Islam, or Christianity. It is alarming that there are this many people here on earth claiming to practice only three ways of living. One thing is for certain they do not practice the same way of living, even within the same religion, each of them have sub groups which have their own norms. Though this is true, many religions remain connected through their similar moral codes.

The Golden Rule with the 13 most popular religions in the Earth is summed up as "Treat others the way you want to be treated". This is God's message and the Law of Attraction because it states anything you give will be returned to you. We are exposed to a Universal Law meaning that it transcends earth into the cosmos. Any energy released in the universe will be continuously returned as it came to be after being received. The cycle simply goes; circles have no beginning or end, they are one in the same always.

Becoming your most spiritual and mental self, intertwining with the Higher Power to become the most evolved in the body is the goal, I've learned. Your job is figure out what is going on. Who are you? What can you do? What is pleasing? What is discomforting? What is ecstasy? You exist in more than one aspect, as you exist in *one* aspect. Like God, right? Father, Son, Holy Spirit; Spiritual, Mental, Physical; Spirit, Mind, Body.

Your job while in the *body* is to understand how to transcend the body. Using spiritual wisdom and mental aptitude one can understand dimensions and how to travel. We need to figure out humans' capabilities before we begin to build; I'm thinking we may be more advanced then we suspect. I think of ancient cultures, living a simpler lifestyle so they had the opportunity to harness their true potential. Notice how their cultures' monuments are still standing, they knew something. They reached a level of consciousness that Man today dreams of but simply doesn't recognize the opportunity to grow and evolve.

    To transcend we must go beyond fear demonstrating pure Faith, pure Energy, and receive the blessing of evolving into a greater being. You must go beyond fear but for you to, understand what you are dealing with. Fear has many faces: guilt, dishonesty, pessimism, envy, the list goes on, but knowing more about the many forms of fear will lead you to conquering each one becoming fully faithful and knowing Love in its purest form. To become faithful in love, we must be able to believe in something inside of ourselves.

This belief is best rooted in God, the Universe, or simply the process of Life. Understanding our place in the grand scheme as we discover who we are, giving us a clue as to what we are to do while here. Our purpose is rooted in faith, demonstrating faith reveals our reason for being. Faith is our spiritual strength that we need to rely on, as it knows no bounds. Knowing we are always Good, no matter the circumstances, is one of the first steps in the journey.

Faith is knowing everything works itself out in the end. I'm sure you have heard that said before but couldn't fathom *the how*. In different terms, your definite thoughts, feelings, and expressive ways being heavily rooted in positivity will yield positive results. Demonstrating strong faith means being able to continue shining brightly even though you may be the only source of Light present. You are all you need and by You, I mean the Higher Self which is identical with God. Aligning with the Higher Self is knowing God which is to know Love.

Love is expressed as a vibration which is simply waves of a frequency, to be more specific 528Hz. As for the dwelling place, the Mind is where Love is housed, also the Heart center so it's no coincidence that the brain and heart are connected. Thoughts occur in the brain and feelings in the heart, but they do find themselves mixing it up a bit. I'm pretty sure you've heard of thinking with your heart and the right brain being associated with feeling.

Most importantly, out of Love came life, it's all sound at different frequencies; sound is at the basis of all materialization. You can't hear love, but you can feel love, because Love is Energy in the form of Frequency indicated by Vibrational waves.

Love is one of the highest vibrations signifying it as one of the highest mental states. Additionally, Thoughts and Feelings formed in love will manifest as prosperity because your intent is god-like. Many are typically only conscious of romanticized and family love but become aware of Self Love. This is the most powerful aspect of *love* as it is a fuel for you that is infinite. If you love You, everything will be good. In doing so, realize who you are and how to care for at least yourself.

Learning who you are allows you to make peace with the not so pleasant details about you, also providing you with the ammo to combat the negatives with positives.

For instance, Numerology gives great depth into who we are as individuals, which we will cover later. Love is a lot of things and can be explained many ways but all in all *love* is *life*.

To be better at living we must learn from those who came before us. All of the prophets showed us how to have *faith* in the process, *love* ourselves and neighbors, along with demonstrating *discipline* throughout the journey. Buddha, Moses, Muhammad, Lao Tzu, Yahshua, etc., they all delivered similar messages; care about one another, believe in one another and stick by one another.

Notably, unity is the highest realm as the purpose of *life*, I've learned, is to become One. Deserving of more, as one we are capable of more making our task unifying the Body, Mind, and Spirit to transcend dimensions. Unity allows for more creation as we maximize pleasure and minimize pain; so far, being conditioned for the challenges up ahead is the best way to be. Being unified is Supreme, energized by Faith, Love, and Discipline.

Also, note that Discipline is of the body and we exemplify it in the way we choose to live. We are to live righteously meaning in right standing with God which can be summed up in the Ten Commandments, the Tao Te Ching, or any other reference to proper living. These are two resources I refer to providing insight, they give me what I need to continue. Everything referenced is relevant, comprehensible, and achievable, so following the them will lead one on a journey of self-discovery resulting in a prosperous life.

No, it will not be easy, as the world is run by negativism only wanting your soul to be as dark as it. Be cognizant, as darkness is a part of *nature* whether you believe or not and honestly nonbelievers are the easier targets because they are more likely to drift. Resist the negative forces that are at bay waiting for you to delve into their world. Sure, some make it back into the Light but why risk it when you already know the guidelines to life.

My generation tends to look at Holy Books as a restriction on fun when, in fact, they are guardrails. Meaning, they inform us on how our behavior determine our experience in this life and the one thereafter. Holy Books are never to be perceived as your ceiling, as they do not place limitations on you, but they do state what's at stake if we do not master discipline.

Typically, disciplined individuals seek very little in terms of materials. Then, there are some that want for nothing yet receive everything showing that we don't need what we want. If you had everything you ever wanted, you wouldn't know what to do next because many wants are rooted in worldly possessions. When we're focused on the creations of man, we lose sight of the worm. That's what the Holy books represent, good places to invest energy, identifying darkness, and how to overcome the dangers that lurk.

Unfortunately, since we, my generation, have been spoon fed information, we expect someone to teach us in order to learn. I disagree with the idea of being fed after a certain point in maturation, feed yourself by reading through material for yourself to better understand. When you read it, you live it. Recognize this as it aids in your betterment. Understanding doesn't magically happen, you must want it and ask for it; like the wisest of them all, King Solomon, who was granted wisdom after asking for it. Learning from him, I prayed for wisdom and understanding in 2013-2014 and what followed were *experiences* to say the least.

First, my family was evicted from our home, which may seem harsh but at the time I completely understood and was ready to leave. It was too much house for the four of us, only occupying three of five bedrooms. I mentioned to my family beforehand that we needed to downsize because I recognized too much money was being invested incorrectly. As the circumstances changed, we were to evolve into greater versions of our previous selves. My older brother got married and started his family. And since we didn't evolve, we were pushed to anyway.

At this point, I elected to stay with a close friend versus my grandmother because I knew I would have the freedom to delve into the darker realm of *smoking* cannabis and having my lady at the time stay as I pleased. This is the time I began my college career which I expected to be exciting, but I will return to that *story* later. As time progressed at my friend's cousin's home, I had my fair share of opportunities. It was like a halfway house to the real world, the freedoms of your own place with the security of a place to sleep. This was my time to learn what it takes to survive, and cannabis assisted during my consistent *"L's"*.

The "*L*" that shook me a bit was a break up, before I realized how pivotal it was in my development. However, having what you feel is the love of your life tell you, no matter the choice of words, they can no longer invest energy into you is earth shattering. It felt like I was given up on by one of the few who understood who I was, where I was going, and for the life of me, I couldn't figure out why.

Confused and conflicted with negative thoughts and insecurities, I wasn't accepting a break from my relationship because I had seen others take breaks, which only resulted in testing the waters with other individuals and I wasn't having it. After gaining some sense of confidence, I remember smoking a blunt and calling her to explain that I was misunderstanding what was happening.

Of course, by this time my number had been deleted but because of the effects of cannabis I was able to put my pride and insecurities to the side to accept the changes I was experiencing. This still just the beginning of my transformation.

Also, at the time, I was driving a 1987 Nissan Maxima which my step dad bought for me a couple years prior. This car needed a lot of work done to it, but I was up for the challenge expecting assistance when needed. Needless to say, I never received assistance because the circumstances changed dramatically, to point no one could've predicted it.

This '87 Maxima was taking me through it, but I knew it was all I had so I remained faithful. I knew if the car was running in tip top shape it'd be a gem, only problem is it was never in tip top shape. I invested over two thousand dollars of my own money to fix a car that was never fixed. The same wheel came off two times while driving and nearly a third. The battery died several times while I was in class, and my dad was always coming through in the *clutch* with help.

When I needed him most he showed up every time, paying to get parts fixed, getting the car towed, everything. I really do appreciate him for showing me that when he's willing, able, and capable of being a father. I learned a lot during my stint of driving a vehicle that's older than me.

Notably, the whole experience led me to trust my dad's decision making more, so we ended up scraping the car for three hundred dollars. After the ordeals of 2014, in 2015, I ended up receiving a 2013 Ford Taurus because I agreed to drive for a ride-share company seeing as my dad was doing it and feeding his family just fine.

Although a fun experience, at the time my discipline wasn't up to par and my dad would consistently let me know I wasn't doing enough. He knew that I smoked and suspected that it was the reason behind my laziness, although I sternly disagreed. The day I had enough of his mouth was a day I should've been working, yet I preferred to smoke. I decided to ride after yet another call from him to intensify my *fire*, because I had to prove him wrong. I wasn't some bum pothead, but I needed to have much better priorities.

As a result, on this very day I damaged my car picking up a client in the heart of Atlanta; talk about *energy*, working with a vengeance and I receive another *L*.

It begins with me missing a turn in 5 o'clock traffic so I turned on the next street. I called the client, but she was unwilling to walk less than three minutes to my vehicle, so I had to do a huge turn around just to get another attempt to pick her up. As I approached my turn this time, I noticed it was a tight squeeze. There was a car exiting the college and traffic behind me, so I made the decision to take the turn anyway, scraping the rear passenger side of my car.

By far one of the worst days, not to mention that by the time I dropped the lady off, my brother and my mother were blowing my phone up. My dad called them both to tell them I was into cannabis, but my mother didn't believe him. For this reason, I said nothing to disagree with what her notion that my dad was crazy for even thinking that I was smoking although I knew his words were true. Because she didn't ask if I smoked, I didn't admit that I did. I felt guilty and ashamed that all of this could've been avoided had I been more focused.

As I calmed myself, I returned my brother's call. He spoke from a different perspective, from the dangers of dealing drugs although that was not my case. I wasn't a drug dealing, nevertheless I did indulge in cannabis. Meaning, I was around drug dealers What's done in darkness shall come to light.

Then, I got into an accident about a month later, a week before my second year of college and luckily totaled my car. I couldn't make the next payment anyway, nor did I want to pay to get the Atlanta scrape fixed. Since I was driving for a ride-share company and had a passenger in the car, everything was handled by my employer's insurance versus mine.

No one was injured, although I did manage to hit three cars because I wasn't being as attentive as I needed to be. Being that the lane I was in, the *fast lane* had completely stopped but the others were still moving, I didn't think to come to a stop. I'm thinking they would be moving again by the time I reached them and was wrong, paying the price.

At the last minute, I attempted to swerve into the HOV lane, but I was a little too late. I hit the first car on the left bumper, as the side of my car continued to scrape the first, I swing back in and hit the second car. Then the momentum of the car brings it forward to scrape the third car.

I was in complete disbelief that I had yet another *L* to endure. My instincts kicked in and I immediately got out of the car because there was smoke entering my car through the vents. By the time a State Farm truck arrived, we realized the car needed to be pushed to a safe area by their truck. My sincerest apologies that I caused an inconvenience for everyone involved, especially my passenger who was in route to a business meeting.

Since my credit worsened before I returned to the dealership to get a new vehicle, I was unable to get the same car. However, a 2012 Ford Fusion isn't half bad. My credit worsened because during the time I was paying to get the Maxima fixed, I was acquiring credit cards to buy the *things* I wanted. In total, maxing out 4 credit cards upwards to almost two thousand in debt. Not only did I max out the credit cards but not making the payments led to each of them going into collections creating derogatory marks on my credit. Derogatory marks have a significant effect on the credit score. I'm realizing today, I attracted all of that to happen to me by not living right. It's safe to say I've learned what it feels like to receive consistent *L's*.

With the Fusion, I began to understand discipline with driving, but it came a little too late as the car was repossessed due to a week late payment. I didn't know the company would be so strict, but the salesman did warn me by saying "make sure your first few payments are on time to establish a good relationship". The repossession happened the very next day after my major revelation, *the awakening*.

As I'm driving home, *high*, after buying more cigarillos, it finally hit me why the Bible is authentic. I struggled to understand how it's considered God's Word, yet men wrote it. Well, God speaks through people, revealing to them what they are to do and how to go about doing it. Seeing my life flash before me, it revealed how often my steps were directed.

Also, it's no coincidence that I was to be relieved of my car the next day, the week of Christmas. In the moment, I accepted it because I was aware that change needed to happen, but I didn't know that everything had to change immediately. These experiences were my first glimpses as an adult of Faith, Love and Discipline: the trinity.

Without a car, I was left to do what others wanted because I didn't feel I had much say so. Part of me didn't mind but the *true* me knew the experiences weren't for me. I never complained, I just kept moving as if nothing had changed. Come to think of it, I wasn't very attached to much at the time because everything left just as quick as it came, and I always knew "it's all good".

Yes, I went to church a bit and enjoyed the experiences. I even got *saved*, meaning I accepted Yahshua as Lord and Savior. Although I didn't attend church often, I was sure to continuously receive their messages, but I knew for me, going to church on a regular basis would feel like a job if I genuinely had no desire to be there. The beginning of me saying "No", a lesson coming from my mother.

One night she texted me saying I woke her up out of her sleep and was wondering if I was okay. I knew then that I had to be honest and say no. I informed her that I was being pulled in directions I had no desire to be in and she told me straight up that I must start saying no. This was tough for me at the time as I didn't want to disappoint anyone, but I was always the one left disappointed in the end. This conversation couldn't have come at a better time, thank you God.

Following, my confidence grew in my actions so if I didn't want to partake I got better at denying opportunities. This lead me to spending more time with my mom whenever I had the opportunity. Also, she'd let me drive her car, just to keep money in my pocket. Lovely lady.

Eventually I was being evicted again because I couldn't afford to pay what I owed to live there. So, I moved back in with my parents and immediately after moving in, I drifted away from college and more into the

Bible. I would read, study and watch sermons on the daily; back to Faith, as I rediscover what work truly is. Yes, we humans are here to work but what is work?

Working is feeding, clothing, and sheltering your family and yourself. This process does not require money, it requires time and energy. Going from, thinking that I wanted to be in corporate America due to job and financial security, to my life changing after learning the simplicities I desire are attainable. I had finally found my purpose, to spread God's message, now only I had to learn what that meant.

First, I thought it meant simply teaching others about the Bible but I received nothing telling me to be a pastor. Needing to experience more, I received a job at the company of my choosing in the airport. Six to seven months after being hired I was promoted to supervisor over my previous role.

Having conversation with coworkers led me here, writing a book, as it was suggested to me by *one* who simply listened. Not only to what was said, but how it was said, and even listening to what wasn't said, allowing Truth to be revealed to him. He saw in me what I had no clue existed, leading me on a more urgent journey of Truth, reigniting my fire, sending me everywhere for answers. As you can tell, the cycle repeats itself, Faith, Love, Discipline.

So far, I've noticed there needs to be a raise in the level of accountability in religious communities, specifically the Christian community. There's a disconnect between the melanated *being* and the church, especially with the millennial generation. We are taught that we received the Bible as slaves after everything else of our heritage was stripped so we need clarification on the timeline. Furthermore, we need to be taught in terms of today, just who the characters of the Bible are. For instance, Hebrews are melanated while the Gentiles would represent Caucasians. The skin tone of Jesus or Yahshua was explained in the Book of Revelation. His complexion was also confirmed when his family fled to Egypt to live amongst the Egyptians during His childhood.

Hold your pastors accountable, your church leaders, hold your brothers, sisters and **most** importantly yourselves accountable. Church leaders need to uplift their people and tell them who they are; let them know the Bible is a book written by them for them, *melanated beings.*

Often, I wonder why many Christian pastors of color do not preach about the complexion of characters in the Bible. These days I'm beginning to realize it is because the Christian church in America is the dominant society's method of worship, not ours. If we are to be knowledgeable on the Word, we must tell of the true color of these people, our people. Hold the Brown Pastors accountable, ask them for the *whole* Truth not just part of it.

Now, I'm sure we can all agree that the Holy Bible holds a dear message but what we will not do is say you must be a 'Christian to be righteous'. What you are to do is outlined in The Good Book, summarized as, be disciplined in the Body because there are traps created by negative forces awaiting your arrival. Since you will need assistance, call on the One who has Lived, Died and Risen Again. He who showed that it is possible to uphold the Law and sacrificed himself to ensure we always have a home in the heavens. Demand Truth and live with it.

Enlighten congregations by sharing Truth with them about the Bible. Therefore, more sun people would invest in churches if leaders didn't preach to get the most money. *These* pastors are business and marketing executives, living off your seed, so sow in those who lead you to feeling conviction. More of our brown pastors should advertise how they invest their earnings into community central banks as well. Instead some are pouring money into banks that give melanated beings a hard time upon requesting a loan. We too, as individuals, need to invest our funds into banks that are for our communities and not looking to capitalize off our misfortunes.

Also, why is it that a lot of white churches participate in missionaries, which may be a slight exaggeration to my experience while working at the Atlanta airport. Only a slightly because there's a sprinkle of melanin in a few of the groups I saw going to Latin American and Caribbean countries. And they always go to melanin rich countries too, like: Caribbean, Africa, Central and South America, that's the odd part. To me, it doesn't look right after learning the history of Europeans traveling, conquering, in the name of Jesus. Teach your congregations instead of selling half-truths and promises.

Some pastors expose us to just enough Truth to get us back in next week, they don't teach us to the point where you want to explore the Word for our own Truth. There's so much present in the Bible to help but they limit our perspective on it by not shedding light on a couple specifics.

One, that we are *the* Israelites, *the* Hebrews, as "African Americans", even though we aren't first generation Africans living in America. And two, the events in the Bible transcend religion as a subject. I wonder if the leaders even know these things to be true themselves. It becomes a reflection of the institutionalized learning instilled, only being thought of as a commodity because we rarely learn what we came for. We must learn the specifics but the lens it's told through isn't the complete Truth.

Churches would benefit greatly if the teachers drew their wisdom from more than one resource. I believe they do but they do not provide the alternative resources; if they did many in their audience would grasp more concepts within the Bible and apply them. Many in attendance, I've realized, focus solely on the pastor, and look to him/her to provide all clarity. But I'm here to pose the question, if the audience always go to leaders for clarity, when does the audience retrieve clarity on their own?

Ministers, Pastors, and Bishops alike do a good job of interpreting the Bible, but I often wonder how to make the experience better. How to transcend generations to continue leading our people to prosperity, not continuously return to support the leaders' personal endeavors. Our people need to learn to remove all middle men and speak directly to God themselves.

I do understand that God will speak through His people, but I also recognize that the traditional version of church isn't as fulfilling as it's intended to be. The lessons can be sporadic, or the leaders simply need to step it up. There needs to be a transcendence between the information presented and the knowledge the pastors have acquired throughout the years. These are principles that other godly men understood, expansion of consciousness.

We can talk about Buddha too, who explained he was a regular guy yet able to be in tune with the Divine Source to reach nirvana. Buddha is indeed an individual to become familiar with. Nirvana is a state of pure bliss reached when one is no longer attached to anything, not even their own ego. I'm not sure where all the buddha statues, figurines, trinkets, and other *worldly* possessions came from but I don't agree with them.

After learning from an ex-Satanist, that there are dark spirits dwelling inside of figurines, I lost interest in all creative statues depicting beings. But then again if there can be dark spirits, there can be light. Even so, I still don't condone worshipping a material. Vanquish your attachment to all material possessions as Buddha did to become a Buddha, or enlightened one, released of worldly tethers.

Even Lao Tzu was only a man, but he achieved high states in consciousness and made a change in the life he was going to live. Living during a time of chaos and wars in 500BC, Lao Tzu elected to live a different way and wrote a book about the experience. The Tao Te Ching is a 5000-word book. Inside are the keys to life and the workings of the universe. Much of which needs to be reflected on because simplicity always comes with depth.

The book is the basis of Taoism, a religion based on you finding your own way as it acknowledges that everyone has their distinct path. Tao meaning *the way*, signifying everyone is so unique that there are over 7 billion paths to righteousness.

At some point in Life we are responsible for our own *doing*. Since this is true, we must be responsible because life comes down to management. We must manage it seeing that we are always spending our original currency, time. Everyone speaks of all they want to do but the issues ensue when prior obligations interfere with new ones. The thing is, that's manageable, you control how you spend your time. Maybe not initially because you may be punished by an authoritative figure if you rebel but over time you are granted more access to manage. So, until you know what is best for you learn what is best for you.

Study how to manage living; how to eat, how to meditate, how to cultivate, how to build, how to establish, and how to live. In other words, innerstand all the information because it only becomes useful when it is applied to your life. The knowledge you acquire has the capability of transcending time to be everlasting wisdom passed down. The wise use what they have, so use the tools accordingly.

Moreover, the illusion created in *money*, or this item summoned to divert the masses' attention, is leaving people running on a treadmill with food dangling in their face. Keeping the people heavily focused on everything except themselves which drains their energy to fuel (((their))) creation. That is what (((they))) have been doing for centuries; shifting the reality we experience by altering our mentalities. Projecting negativity on us will eventually catch up because the system only lasts if those doing the leg work are solely focused on the material realm.

Likewise, we are taught to neglect our minds and spirits, keeping us tied up in our day to day duties. Removing the spirit and mind from a person leaves us an empty shell susceptible to any and all influence. This concept I like to refer to as drifting, which leaves us molded by the visuals released by the media industry. They exist to sway our thoughts to become fear-based creating dependency.

Notably, we the people usually don't get the opportunity to discover our specific line of work because of our dependency of systematic structures. Everyone is here to do more within the body which requires incorporating our minds and spirits. We are here on earth to work, yes, but that does not include clocking in and out. We must change our mindsets to recognize Truth. If a company, your employer, is not interested in the betterment of the planet, they cannot be trusted. If they don't care to improve the environment, then they don't care for your well-being either. It's rare to find a company that isn't fixated on cash; seeing as that is the purpose for a business: to create revenue and earn profit. Which leads me to another question, what's the purpose of making money?

I've learned that learning how to make money does not equate to learning how to live. Many people associate money with opportunity; more money, more opportunity and this couldn't be further from the Truth. Money is but another resource and like all resources, comes and goes.

There's no need to seek deeply for financial stability because financial stability is heavily rooted in discipline. But our system isn't structured to truly teach society about how to live effectively and efficiently.

One doesn't secure discipline, a key to effective living, by obtaining more. One must gain discipline before more comes. Before discipline, one will be attached to a resource and the result of attachment being suffering. So, without discipline one is suffering, feeling without yet, one has everything necessary to continue. Once you recognize that you are Good, that you are indeed a child of God capable of anything you can imagine, create opportunities, seize them, and progress to the next. The result of being disciplined to the guiding of the Spirit.

As we progress through Life with the Spirit, we realize the phases of life are literal and we only move on after we've learned. Meaning, we will continuously be faced with the same issues until we solve the initial problem. Say for instance that the root of a problem is a lack of Love exuded, we will endure endless experiences where the lacking is made apparent. For example, how war, bigotry, and hatred are rooted in fear, Love's opposite. These types of revelations only come with we are a union with the Spirit.

Retaining supreme confidence in our connection with cosmic energy leads us toward Love, only that which spews Life. A fancy way of saying, with the Spirit, or Faith in God leads us where He needs us. Whatever doesn't naturally facilitate *life* is not conducive to nurturing us as we learn, a necessity for thriving. Lessons are the key to learning, and a lesson is simply a concept to be taught or learned. Indeed, teaching and learning are one in the same but alternate extremes, different phases of the cycle. No matter the phase in the cycle of *life*, it's all *love* driven.

Regardless of which religion you practice, model yourself after the *being* most spoken about, the one leading with Love. The central figures are the example of how to move through life disciplined and in tune with the Higher Power. Discipline allows you keep what you receive. Too often my people, receive what they need and want but soon lose it due to a lacking in discipline. Correct the errors of the past as you keep strong Faith, live in Love, and sustain with Discipline. Each religion has some form of faith, love, and discipline mentioned.

Discipline yourself to operate more in Love, and eventually all you will exude is Love. Anything you release will be returned, so release Love unconditionally, *be* as those who came before you. In any case, the higher you vibrate, the more love you exude, the more opportunities at success you have. More doors present themselves when you broadcast your frequency more, thus higher vibrations attract more. Love is one of the highest vibrations you can vibrate on. Project love even to yourself to empower your physical body.

Mastery of the physical body, the temple, is imperative for a successful life, which means caring for the one vessel you are to operate in. Our bodies are majority water so be sure to drink plenty of it! This is coming from a guy who, as a kid, would gag forcing myself to drink water.

Drinking more water will lead you to correcting other impurities within the body as well because water has healing properties. Drinking more water is a way to practice discipline and display to you that you are capable of so much more. The journey can be grueling so Faith in the process is necessary. Do it for you but for more as well, it is a balancing act required for desired manifestation.

Mom BDay Poem

Becoming everything you saw in me
Majestic, brilliant, loving
Graceful, tranquil
I still have to show you something
What happens when you are free

I AM The One
Fueled by the Son
And guided by the Moon
It still feels too soon

Keep going
But keep growing
And I will continue showing
What you have shown me

Chiles play

They wake up feeling like everyday
Is a new day to play
Not to do what someone say
As if you don't have a childish way
Or two
Don't confuse Remember
Being a kid in September

Manifestation

Who knew I would write a book in 2011? Going from creating a blog as an exit portfolio in AP Literature to a book with the same title six years later, talk about manifesting. I didn't have the slightest idea what the title of the blog would amount to, in fact, I didn't even know what to title my blog! To this day, I do not feel that I can take credit for the title because it came in the form of revelation. A voice spoke to me and said, "path to righteousness", and at the time I initially spelled righteousness incorrectly. I wasn't sure if it was God speaking through me or if the innermost me was surfacing.

Looking back on it I see, the key to manifesting is asking the *right* questions to get the *right* answers. After I graduated, I remember having one of many sleepless nights, so I decided to jot down all the questions I had. Question after question stemming from my lacking to innerstand God which caused confusion inside of me because I didn't know where to go.

Following a Path of Righteousness will lead you to your anointing, your God given abilities, or your gift, however you wish to refer to it, it's all the same. When we stray from what's right, we are left relying on natural abilities to tackle supernatural occurrences. It's no longer a fair fight without the Spirit; we are experiencing Spiritual warfare and you need your Spirit activated to shift into your Higher Being.

Ascension into the Higher Self will guide you into efficiently leading themselves toward prosperity and joy. How? The law of Hypnotic Rhythm is a concept coming from *Outwitting the Devil*, meaning you are locked in to a specific behavior permanently based on your dominating thoughts. What does *that* look like? Retaining thoughts of Success, Joy, Bliss, Efficiency, Prosperity, and Love will create a new pattern of habit. Exude these qualities as you journey, and you'll find that Life is a much better experience. Not only must you speak with definiteness, but you must release what you plan to receive.

Innerstand that you are not conformed to your Body, you are an eternal being using this vessel to accomplish a task. You find out what that task is, your purpose, or Dharma, when you begin to innerstand your Source. After you accept the Source and connect, then you will have access to a Higher Realm where you consciously create the world you live in.

Without the Spirit, you unconsciously create the world around you through fear because the enemy doesn't take time off. Whether you know it or not there are dark forces working against you. The sooner you accept this, the sooner you can learn how to defend yourself and even go on the offensive side, because everything naturally yields to God.

First things first, we must understand prayer, our power source. Prayer is the method of materializing your dreams, making the unseen, seen. It does not mean asking for something, but simply the host (you) speaking to create their desired reality. Also, as a collective it's much more powerful, hence the phrase 'strength in numbers'. "Again I say to you that if two of you agree on earth concerning anything that they ask, it will be done for them by My Father in heaven. For where two or three are gathered together in My name, I am there in the midst of them."

Matthew 18:20. A couple of key verses where Jesus was explaining the power in collectivism. He was explaining how much power we have in agreement no matter what we say regardless if it's positive or negative.

Whether we are conscious of what we say or not, the words we utter shape our future. Praying is about realizing how small you are yet how powerful you can be. Know too, that you can influence what your fate is by the words you release and the actions that follow. One who prays understand that s/he is not the one who determines destiny but can influence what comes next with prayer.

I have always known of prayer but nowadays, my perspective has expanded into everything I emit as a form of prayer because I receive all that I release into the Universe. As a child growing up being affiliated with

Christian churches, I'd take on their definition of prayer, conversing with God, asking for something. Never asking for materials, more so intangibles such as strength, guidance, wisdom, and understanding, and I did just that up until adulthood.

After I graduated high school, I remained unsure about what to pursue in life, so I began to pray. All I asked for was to be showered with the Spirit of wisdom and understanding. Over the years, since then, I've had my eyes open wider than I could've ever imagined. As my awareness grows, I also know that I am still only beginning to see.

It wasn't until I created my own website, weRICHeous.com, that I discovered how vast prayer is. Learning how to manifest through my speech by repeating affirmations that guarantee my wellness, I created my own affirmation: I Am Healthy, I Am Wealthy, I Am Full of Love. Saying this throughout the day ensures your needs are met and that you are giving others what they need most.

Affirmations help immensely along your walk of Faith. They remind you that you can impact your always destiny with the words you utter, the thoughts consistently on your mind, and the feelings deep within your heart. Be cognizant of your energy, the vibrational frequency you emit, because this determines what you attract on your path. Given these points, ensure your prayers are bringing about positive change in and around you. Prayer is when you are intentional and specific requesting what you need to experience. Which is why you should be mindful that what you ask for, you will get, as long as you believe you receive it.

Now, take manifestation to the next level because we must protect us, but first we must learn protection on every level; spiritual, mental, and physical. Take on the personal challenge of maintaining you, that's your first duty. Figure out how to care for You. What does it take to consistently feel Good? That's the first question you ask yourself, speaking to the Universe, or to God, at this point we should know they are one in the same. Now that you have asked aloud, meditation must ensue to receive the revelation on which actions to take next.

For us to understand what's next, *the how*, we must practice meditation. Meditation is a process where a *being* quiets their Mind through steady, calm, deep breathing. For those new to meditation, focus solely on your breathing. As the shift occurs, steadily inhale, pause, exhale, pause, and repeat; you will notice the flow. The flow of Life within you, the ether flowing in and around you will present fresh, authentic ideas and ideals for you to pursue. This is a revelation; another aspect of the plan being revealed to you.

Utilize your spiritual and mental advantages but remember that you still may access physical knowledge in the form of past events to learn from as well. Looking back on Black Wall Street, their only flaw was no physical protection. Which is understandable because how were they supposed to know that Americans would perform the first airstrike on their own soil at that time. It was a major lesson that we should all take heed to, never underestimate the adversary, and come back better.

We create our own living, so be sure to create out of Love to *live* the life you want. However, know if you are living immoral nothing will work. The way to know if you are living immoral is by assessing your living situation, because your physical realm is a reflection of your mental realm which is the result of spiritual balance/imbalance. The stronger the spirit the more it can be relied upon to guide decisions.

We as *light beings* must help everyone realize any energy harnessed is that which we choose to harness. We must accept this truth before we elevate, because whatever we *choose* to accept as real becomes as real as it's made to be. Embrace all, conscious of the energy you receive, as well as the energy you release to surrounding life. We all exchange energy with one another, so we must realize that if we wish for our environment to reflect health and wellness, we must project that into the Universe.

Today, we need more leaders to manifest positive realities, but many want to be a boss because a lot of bosses do not work. We don't need any more bosses, we need to look within and recognize our Inner Guide as life continues. The Inner Guide only wants what is best for you but beware, because that isn't the only energy force within able to sway your steps and influence reality.

Along the journey to becoming a master at manifesting, you'll develop the ability to distinguish energy. After you acknowledge identity, learn how to harness, and share your wisdom with the next. Leaders uplift their support to be their equal, understanding the proverb, "a chain is only as strong as its weakest link".

Bosses are only concerned with the amount of power and influence they themselves hold, seek to be a leader. Leaders are *beings* that use their ultimate gift, their mind, in accordance with the Higher Power to facilitate bliss.

We understand that the mind is very powerful, even though it is not the Source; it's more of a generator because thoughts are generated whether you intend to think or not. The *mind* is a heart and brain union becoming *one*, but to access what? The Third Eye, a spiritual bridge in the mind, connecting us to an energy *source* such that it aligns the body, unifying the trinity to become One.

The body goes as the Spirit and mind lead. The spirit leads while the mind intensifies the sensations formed, guiding our bodies toward the goal. The spirit never rests; although you can wish for mental rest, a simple detox is rejuvenating, so empty your mind. Unfortunately, the body does need rest to be fully functional, which is why many recommend at least 7 hours of sleep daily. It allows the body to freely interact with the Spirit and Mind to correct any imbalances within. As imbalances are corrected you will begin to recognize the *being* deep within.

As you observe what you are naturally attracted to, you are learning who you are. Become aware of all that you enjoy, all that gives you *life*. Beware though, there are entities that feed on light. Many are conscious about a multitude of things they do not like because they draw inspiration from the outside in, but creation begins from within as the environment nurtures.

Look within to feel more, think about more to innerstand who you are. Today many are persuaded to think about what they want to do before they have learned who they are and what they are capable of. This is by design, if you don't know who you are then you can be convinced of anything.

Your mind's readiness to shift will lead you to attracting more lessons and confessions. What you encounter in the physical realm will be processed in the mind; learn from it so you can move on. The more you learn, the more disciplined in the body you can expect to be, but our learning must be beneficial to growth.

Allow the body to enlighten you on your condition knowing when it's necessary to follow it. There must be a will to walk with discipline in the natural realm because disorder in the mind leads back into the body as a lack of health. Lack of physical health does not directly impact the spirit; however, everything is connected.

When the mind and body are not functioning in tip top shape, the initial reaction is to try to fix it. This takes our attention away from the spirit or Higher Self, instead we lead with the Ego in decision making resulting in a weakened spirit only because it is neglected. When the Spirit isn't in use it can no longer power the mind to control the body, and you cannot control your mind without spiritual strength due to a lack of connection to your Higher Self. Connect with the Higher Self or Cosmic Energy to begin your journey of discipline so you can accomplish more.

Nevertheless, be prepared, the more in-tune you become with yourself the more sensitive your senses become. Many aren't prepared for these intense feelings, but we must remember that just because they occur does not require us to act. Our only action shall be to let the *feelings* or mere energy flow freely. Praise your sensitivity because at this stage you are truly connected to the quantum field of energy.

I learned this on my own as I received knowledge on the supernatural realm from different resources. It took a few years of free learning to lead me to the discoveries of what sensitivity is. We notice the slightest shifts, so we are to remain at peace despite what we feel. Allow what's beyond you to remain beyond until your energy encompasses the negative. Until you know the energy is light, be cautious when it comes to contact as you increase your influential range.

Slight digression, I have a theory about feelings. What if a feeling is from the future or past? It's said that anxiety is rooted in focusing too heavily on the future but what if you are uneasy because the excitement is really from your future self. You feel discomfort intensely in the moment, knowing it's real because of what you *plan* to do, but do you know that you are aligned with your future self now. Which further asserts that our concept of time is one to be adjusted.

On the other hand, when one focuses too heavily on the past, it leads to depression; not being able to enjoy the present moment because of what you have experienced. As you cope with feelings of pain from the past, you may notice the reaction you're experiencing is because it's all in the Mind now. Once you forgive for the events of the past, you can move forward, and yes you can forgive and remember. Maintaining balance in the mind is about being *present*, rooted in the now, what can you do right now?

Whenever you are along your journey, consistently ask what can be done, what can you manifest at this moment to be better off. We must combine perspectives to complete the perspective such that it is received wholly or Holy, otherwise it can be "holey" to the average person. This is in large part due to teachers leaving education needing restoration on the Spiritual realm, Mental realm, as well as the Natural realm or Material realm.

Everything in the physical realm was created in the Mental realm with power from the Spirit. Since the teachers have been corrupted, we must take our education in our own hands and create again. Although we were nudged to learn on our own, we lacked the necessary inspiration because of how beneficial information appears. We must change the narrative and inspire the next generation to elevate their education, it's the only way we restore our lives.

The spirit is required for restoration as it is the energy source, *Pure Potentiality* as Deepak Chopra says. Pure potentiality is energy ready to fuel any creation, such as a Thought or a Feeling. Use this form of creation in the Mind to manifest at any rate you wish. Each realm has a light/dark side, one cannot be without the other, they are complements. Soften your Heart and become sensitive to your Spiritual signals as you are guided throughout life.

Innerstand your feelings go beyond typical emotions into deep yearnings for better circumstances. Deep within we can feel that better circumstances are attainable, however we must back our definiteness of purpose with a definite plan to achieve a purpose and we'll have success. This philosophy is according to the "devil" in *Outwitting the Devil*. Check it out, you'll receive tons of insight on the realms of energy.

Our heart is a gateway to the Spirit in the form of Love. Love is the gateway to prosperity and happiness and is typically associated with the heart. The Mind fosters and the Spirit is the fuel or life force behind all ideas functioning on faith so **your** ideas only go as far as **you** project them. The amount of energy you invest in directly results in the magnitude of the material you've formed. If you put in a little good you'll receive a little good, if you put a lot then you receive a lot. The same goes for good's opposite. A gateway is created to allow passage, the gateway doesn't choose the energy that enters, you must consciously or unconsciously welcome it.

Whatever you give is what you receive, karma is real and translates into action. Our actions determine our future, one way or another. There must be universal laws even to govern God, seeing as there is some repercussion to all action. If good is done, it is only right that good be done in return. But no one is exempt from *bad* and it's the same for everybody with the difference being the magnitude of the karma.

Some are living the generational effects of their ancestors' decisions, but I come with good news, we retain the power to change our circumstances. Overcome the obstacles to receive that which you deserve, do it for you but include the next as well. Be another great example on how to maintain good Karma and bless your seed for generations to come.

Time is quite the illusion; a concept we agree on because we collectively and individually control it. Time is a phenomenon, as of now, because we all influence the perception without understanding. As children of The Most High, time serves us not the other way around; we witness this when things seem to happen in slow motion or 'time flies' by. The higher our vibrations are, the more conscious we are of our every movement, the more control we have. Learn how to really harness this ability and make it count because you only get one shot....at a time.

This isn't your only shot but it's no telling when you'll get your next shot. So, make it count in this lifetime, it matters, your *life* matters. Learn and progress; make use of time, because it's your original currency, so what you do with what you are given is up to you. You can take the necessary steps to extend your time, but do you really want it. What lengths are you willing to go to for more time? You don't have to do much but recognize your own abilities.

Being *high* to experience this truth is cool but it fades, and I know from experience. Understand who you are at this state of mind and bring it back to your sober reality. The higher you feel while being sober, then the higher your low moments become. Not only that but the mind and body is easier to control when sober. You're freer, high, but at times may be less attentive thus less conscious. You've exploded into this realm of euphoria but lack the discipline to understand that you can access this state 24/7. Some come to this conclusion and take the route of over indulgence, one should instead learn this state and how to achieve it without enhancements. Use it to your advantage and become able to access euphoria sober.

Though while under induced euphoria, I have had the pleasures of receiving more perspective on *natural* occurrences. Telepathic abilities are more common than many realized but typically discovered under stressful circumstances, imagine if you were in a state of euphoria. Everybody has internal voices but what happens if they are others' voices. Have you ever been about to make a decision then hear a loved one's voice either praising or shunning your decision?

They may feel you about to make a pivotal move. The more we connect with one another, the more we are connected, we feel as One. It will be a giant group, but everyone is only connected to whom they have a personal connection with. There's a moral code of privacy which only gives those you trust access and only *God* has complete access, which still must be granted. Everyone else earns access because you house God in the form of your Higher Self providing you with dominion over your mind.

We should be safe among each other before we evolve, which starts with more love because love embraces all. The one aspect of love we specifically need to practice is more Self Love. Everyone is taught to love others but rarely are we taught to think about ourselves.

In some instances, sure we think of self, when forced to care. For instance, if you don't make life style changes you will not have a life to live. You are your first obstacle; learn yourself, truly learn what you are. Innerstand what you are attracted to which will tell you more about who you are. The more you learn about yourself the more you naturally understand another which leads to the safety we need to feel.

As our level of sensitivity to energy has heightened, we must now manage it. Remain cleansed, take precious care of your vessels. It's extremely rare to live in this form, being a human. Sure, life exists on all scales and even planes but in this specific one, you create as you speak. Creating whatever you want with the time you are given to spend, we must understand the duality of us, producers, and consumers. They always throw the consumer label on us, but we are also producers. We can grow our own anything and to create is to produce.

It's imperative to understand balance of our role as producers and consumers for balance in the Earth to be restored. Because we force the pendulum so far left with our lack of care for Earth, She responds through violent natural disasters. We act, She responds. Whatever is done is done, exemplifying the Karmic Law; whatever you do will be done to you.

Don't have expectations either because that will only dim the light on the dream. Now you are focused on making your desires "realistic", whatever that means. To me, it means lessening your own shine by toning down your confidence in yourself to achieve a goal. See what you wish to experience and leave it at that, it will happen so long as you remain focused on it. A key to healing, see yourself already healed, feel well and so you will *be*.

Heal Forreal

How should I feel
What I thought was real
Is part of the deal
They kill and steal meals
But you better not squeal

Still being held accountable
Damages caused
insurmountable
To those that wonder
Remember not to wander

We all know sum
They are everywhere
Only a projection
Nothing to fear
Rise and adhere
Lemme be clear
Danger is real
The option is fear Continue
to abide
By God and I
Not I
But U
Use your I two C through
From you to You
Revealing what is True
That You and you
Are glue

Meeting in the center
In a center
A circle
To work you
May meditate
Or medicate
To levitate
With tones that resonate
With your inner space

Healing

To some it's squirming, some call it moving or dancing, some weird and dangerous, others aligning chakras while straightening the spine, but I call it healing. 5 years prior I was informed of having 'mild to moderate' scoliosis; I still think it's from moving into a larger home earlier in the year, lifting very heavy items improperly.

In 2011, I was frail and if you think I'm small now, then, I was smaller. Due to my shortcomings physically and mentally resulted in me compromising the integrity of my spine lifting an incredibly dense and cheap mattress my brother purchased for his bed. It was unnecessarily heavy, and we had to get it up two sets of stairs with a low clearing. We had to bend this two-foot-thick mattress just to get it under the clearing to make it up the first set of stairs.

My back was hurting immediately after and even worse the day following. Let me be clear, I have never experienced back pain prior. Everybody was saying that it usually doesn't happen like that, it's hereditary but I know what I experienced. Whether my family believed doctors over me was out of my control but I needed healing.

Learning to cope with the consistent pains, I would wear a brace to school or simply hope for a good day. I was told surgery was unnecessary and a back brace would be insufficient seeing as though I was practically done growing taller at 17 years of age. Based upon the size of my hip bone, the doctor saw that I was an adult according to my bone development.

All around were people informing me that I'd have to live with it; the doctor also said that since they were unable to correct my issue, I could strengthen my back muscles along with stretching. He also said that the scoliosis would worsen over time; my assumption is that it was a warning, if I wasn't to take heed to the advice prior. A major lesson of never accepting someone's words regarding my health, unless they are uplifting.

    Fast forward to 2015, I began to practice yoga after conversing of doing so months prior. Drawing inspiration from my uncle who is a certified yoga instructor, I then began to see the masculinity in femininity. One day I decided to stop talking, went to StumbleUpon, looked up yoga, and found the website DoYouYoga. From there I began a 30-day yoga challenge continuing for at least two weeks.

After getting the hang of it, realizing my physical health was indeed improving, I focused on the yoga poses targeting my back. Creating my own regimen, one day I'd do lower and the next upper, then I began to do both upper and lower in the same sitting. Yoga was the beginning of my physical healing where I began to see results.

One night, one of the last if not the last, we were present in the blessing disguised as a lesson, I experienced a miracle. As everyone slept I was experiencing pain in my back, which was met with stretching. Realizing it wasn't helping like it usually would, I laid my back on the floor and began to rock the pain away. This helped more but I still knew more was could be done.

Then I grabbed my waist with a grip so firm it felt like another pair of hands were holding me. As I held tightly, I squirmed upward, only my spine lengthening. At one point, I was certain change was occurring within my body when the *bulge* was on the opposite side. Typically, my right side would bulge out because of the curve in the spine. So, when my left side had the bulge it shocked me, but I quickly gained my composure and continued straightening.

After the pain left, signaling completion, I sat up and my spinal column felt flush for the first time in a long time. So long I forgot what it felt like to feel good, and I felt phenomenal. As I reflected on what just took place it instantly dawned on me that I was being touched by God and I wept. I was engulfed with revelation on why I was there, and everything instantaneously made much more sense.

Since then, I continue to practice yoga periodically. I say periodically because around the same time I understood the value in yoga, I received another job. And the new job became my new form of physical fitness. Continuing to strengthen, my energy would surge whenever smoking a joint, causing tingling in my palms. This was new to me, so I researched, and Reiki energy was what I experienced. Which confirms that I'm a natural healer, I use this energy to continue to heal my body. Mixing reiki healing practices with yoga had become my new regimen, as I endured endless cardio at the job.

Yoga was also not all my regimen consisted of either. I still had a bad habit of smoking. Whenever I would smoke, the energy within intensified. My energy provided me with the ability to shift energy around in my body using my hands and I would dance to remove any discomfort out of my body. Dance is an art form that allows you to feel every ligament in your body; defined simply as rhythmic movements, it is also a form of healing.

The irony of it being the medicine I needed to continue growing as the previous young lady I dated was a dancer. God is beyond interesting when you notice the correlations within your own life. Everything has a purpose and when you discover what it is, your mind will be blown. I utilize all I know to connect the lessons and unlock the ancient wisdom within.

First you experience healing, then you innerstand the entire process. Learning how you healed is the key to continuing. Utilize the energy source which created you to recreate yourself, to heal yourself. Through Love, Faith,

Visualization, and Energy one can be healed of anything, I'm convinced. Yahshua rose from the dead along with resurrecting another prior to. That's power, and used for good, for God.

He has shown all cultures around the Earth what they are capable of in a way they best understand. Energy is all around you, within you from physically to mentally and mentally to spiritually, energy is everywhere. Energy travels in cycles from heart to brain into the mind by way of the pineal gland reaching the spirit realm, it's Source. In the spirit realm, *energy* can either be light or dark and whatever you send into the spirit will be amplified when it returns to the natural.

The body has two natural eyes and a third, a spiritual eye, referred to as the pineal gland. Natural eyes do not realize that which doesn't exist in the physical realm. Your Third Eye is what notices the connections as it is part spirit, in the mind, residing in the center of the physical brain. The Third Eye is at the center of a three circled Venn diagram, with the circles being spirit, mind, and body. Notice how anything of significant importance is typically placed in the center surrounded by protection; which is why the pineal gland is in the center of the brain. The Third Eye is the center and the more you trust the Universe, the more you are placing trust into intuition. Intuition is the Third Eye language, resulting in bodily feelings felt deeper than the body.

Many may not recognize this as a truth, but cannabis is a Third Eye enhancer. So, if your third eye is closed, you are wasting marijuana. However, if you don't elect to experience it but your third eye remains closed, you are no better at being intuitive. Weed aligns you with the Higher Being, leaving you swarmed with thoughts and ideas. It leaves your creativity is at an all-time high, the feeling is truly euphoric. Therefore, many artists indulge in cannabis because the artistic space it introduces you to cannot be duplicated in a sober state.

Feeling like a Super Saiyan mentally, you can think through anything, feeling able to steer the ship more efficiently. Even with this, we must be able to maintain this balance in a sober state. It should take much less to get *high* versus more, which is the typical user. Many simply smoke more to get higher as their tolerance increases, but I've learned that we are to use less as we achieve a high state in waking consciousness. This means that we are *high* sober and *higher* high.

Being high does feel good but if at some point you do not accept the feeling and tap into your abilities, you will waste away. If you are not using your moment to be *high* as an opportunity to unite the three components of the Mind - the conscious, subconscious, and unconscious, you are wasting your time. Unite the compartments of the Mind to be One, granting you access to all, which lasts if you can sustain. Allow the marijuana to naturally cure all ailments within your Body, Mind, and Spirit. As it does its job, do yours and make something happen.

Cannabis allows you to simply Be, but some become "stuck" when they aren't used to the effects. They become absorbed in themselves to the point they do not want to move and end up missing the feeling. After you accept the feeling, you may create freely. You may not feel you can move but you have more access to your Body, Mind, and Spirit. Sure, you can obtain a similar feeling while being sober, but the process requires more work and dedication.

Maintaining a healthy balance is key, eat plenty of fruits and veggies, and remember to drink lots of water. We should at least be able to tolerate food in its healthiest state, fresh from the ground blessed by the Lord. Now that you have eaten you can create more than a meal; the body is fully functional when there is optimal fuel in the tank. After satisfying the Body, it's time to feed the Mind and work through the Spirit with some creations; this is what being human is at its purest form.

Understand how the Life around you lives. Now, enhance it all by maximizing pleasure and minimizing risk. We are here to create better life out of what was given. We are explorers. First, we must explore earth. Furthermore, we do not have to travel far to experience earth because we all live on earth. We must go "outside", which is a very weird term to say the least. The disconnect we have with nature is apparent and must change. There's freedom in nature if you play your role, that of a human being. Obey God, do right, be righteous, and be One with nature harmonizing your frequency with Life. Be free.

You can breathe during anything, it's your ultimate freedom, so always breathe, consciously. Once I realized I was smoking to breathe, I stopped. I was smoking to remain calm, to access and assess feeling, which I learned was possible to accomplish by simply breathing. Breathing in prānā, life, or oxygen is *you* harnessing energy from the original life force. Breathing allows your mind a chance to recognize the corrections needed within the body to reset, that's why sleep is very crucial to health. As you sleep your body is relaxed, you are breathing to gain energy and utilizing it through means of restoration. Allow your body the chance to do what it needs to, so you can remain balanced. As you begin to restore, the sensations may not be as pleasant as expected because there's much to do. The body is practically resetting itself when we take opportunities to simply breathe. Rest assured we come equipped to heal ourselves naturally.

The body is not permanent in any way, shape, or form. It can be molded and sculpted into a work of art.

How much work are you willing to put into yourself to be at your best? Have you discovered what is best for you? I ask because when you take this route there is no material reward. The reward is in the process. Meaning, the fact that you are further along than when you started is the reward. The lessons learned during the journey are the reward. To understand progression as a living being and how to overcome obstacles that are never ending are much more rewarding than the destination.

    Learning must be imbedded in you because the test is ongoing, there's always more. I've learned that I'm curious by nature but wise enough to observe before interaction, wise enough to breathe through all experiences. Breathing is essential to living, if you can breathe through it you can get through it. Utilize your lungs, they are there for a reason.

Feel again! We are taught to neglect feelings, but we need to embrace our feelings. Yes, feelings are emotions which we need to decipher but they also go beyond temporary moments. Feelings are in the Body, Mind, and Spirit. In the body, feelings come in the form of sensations which can be both unique and discomforting. "Gut feelings" are undeniably accurate and we recognize the difference in our physical body telling us to be cautious. We must innerstand what our bodies are telling us we need. We have always acknowledged the changes in our body. For example, as a baby, we would cry with every discomfort and as we grow, we typically cry about less as we embrace our feelings less. To me, embracing feelings is a learned behavior that must be taught.

Before you are distracted in school from learning about who and what you are, you are just beginning to answer the questions within yourself. First becoming aware of behavioral tendencies, which you can either live with or change what you aren't fond of. It must be a conscious personal decision to cycle your energy back into yourself.

Study Self and learn from Self which is God, you'll notice the deeper you go within the more you know about the world around you. First you understand the purpose of God, then, you understand where you come in because Life extends beyond us as individuals, even beyond Earth. I know you can feel the vastness of the Universe within, but I also know that we as a people are callused in pain that must be healed first.

Allow the lungs to expose the pain; where you feel discomfort from expansion and compression of your lungs, send energy there. You must learn to see inside your body through feelings. With power from the Third eye, project energy to an area where you feel discomfort. Pain always fades because we all come with the supernatural ability to restore.

We must now innerstand how to utilize these abilities and consciously achieve the task. It's an adjustment and typically with adjusting, it's a tough process. Only because it isn't immediate, but you must keep going. Noticing the errors is a first step, followed by recognizing your power of change and lastly actual change. A continuous cycle that goes until you realize change is permanent because it is reoccurring. Actively breathing makes one multitask; monitoring the breath and proceeding with daily life is not as easy as it is simple.

Deep breathing must be from the mouth, from the nose we aren't able to absorb as much oxygen. Capable of continuing to survive we must push forward into thriving. Inhaling more air stretches the lungs and the entire diaphragm. There may be discomfort due to imbalances within. For me my back and chest ache from the effects of scoliosis. Although my spine has straightened significantly, the warping of muscle is apparent, due to over compensation in my right hemisphere. At this point I must actively and consciously balance all, firstly within then the exterior follows.

Creation originates from consciousness in the form of frequencies which can transmit life and the absence thereof. All is able to be in tune with creation for all was once created. Healing is an ability formed in spirit harnessed in your mind meaning your essence must be pure to heal. Feel whole, but to do so you must feel all. Feel everything and adjust accordingly removing that which you no longer wish to endure.

For instance, pain, although inevitable, is temporary and will leave as soon as you command it to. Endure the pain as you heal; knowing your tolerance grows as the pain dissolves, you realize Pain is Gain when you overcome it. Elevate beyond pain into Love as Love heals all so you must Love yourself to heal yourself.

Aligning the body is a process that begins with an assessment. Assessing pains and discomforts is the first step. The body is supposed to move, movement should not be an uncomfortable experience. Stretch to loosen your muscles and free up your bones. The Body is moveable, you can shift your body to be in perfect alignment. Breathe!

It is not as easy as it seems, but through everything done, remember to breathe. Inhaling is the work while the exhale is the release. Consciously breathe deeper, and exercise your lungs expanding them to full capacity during your inhale. Many of us are unconsciously holding our breath but that is interrupting the energy flow. Air is a form of energy so let it flow through you.

Breathing allows the healing process to commence, since it is natural the body can re-align. It aides the heart, as the heart pumps blood through your *chosen* vessel. Balance your body as your body balances you. Treat your body like a prized possession because it is the closest thing you'll ever get to truly own. And you only get one physical body at time. So if you're one to believe in reincarnation, you must take care of what you have.

Water is another form of energy, allow it to move you to its rhythm. For me, showers are very therapeutic, erasing all the pain of my body constantly shifting into its proper place. The healing from spinal contusion is a lengthy process, one I didn't anticipate lasting as long. Being in water reminds my body that they are one in the same and the energy flows just as the water flows from the shower head. It's amazing how the pain fades away when the water is placed on the source of the discomfort.

Allow your spirit, mind, and body to be *one* as you breathe. Consistent breathing allows the Spirit to Be as your Mind is awakened and your Body grows. Bodily growth means your body now only retains that which it needs, anything else results in immediate discomfort. A quiet mind is an awakened mind. Keep the consciousness flowing freely without interjection. Let the mind be a mind which is free space. As the spirit properly functions one's intuition will heighten and become more sensitive to the surrounding energy.

Our vibrational frequencies increase as we travel from Body to Mind to Spirit. The Spirit is very similar to air energy thus why change is instant in the Spirit, there's no resistance. The Mind is liquid energy because it can be controlled to some degree or rather it can be guided into a desired direction and when left to flow freely, it will go where it is needed. The Body is earth energy because it is solid yet remains malleable to shifts. Also, because it houses all the elements in the material plane.

Someone to take note of in manipulating the human body is Dr. Sebi who was healing others thought to have incurable illnesses, showing you that you can change at will. You must *know* what to feed it and it will be as you will; beginning as knowledge we first learn of Truth as it pertains to health.

Health is in large part due to knowledge of what we can and cannot eat, the problem in America being, we aren't taught about a proper diet. Sure, we are taught nutrition on some scale but it's all a blatant scheme to attract more money for very specific individuals. Also, if you don't know we are only left with the Spirit of Dr. Sebi as he is no longer with us under very questionable circumstances.

Many have the tendency to disrespect their bodies because they have realized; we can do whatever we want. They feel controlled in other aspects of life, so they utilize the only free place they have. Doing what they want largely because they can. Let's take it further, had they perceived with a macro perspective they would realize that this was the beginning of a universal law. You can do whatever you want.

There are effects for every cause, understand that you determine your own fate. Yes, God knows all, although you remain with the power of choice. You can follow the path laid and make moves or you can do your own thing and remain uneasy. Humans didn't always know of the "other" side. Eating the forbidden fruit became the test of mankind to see if we are worthy of God. Now that we can see both sides of everything that occurs we must choose our path.

Learning from a philosopher by the name of Alan Watts, I am now able to detach myself from myself meaning that I am able to allow my thoughts and feelings to be without interjection or a reaction. I still think and feel deeply frequently only now I seek to understand more. I want to know why I feel in a moment to better understand myself and what really makes me tick. Typically, we feel but cannot articulate why we feel or even what we feel. For me to ask for more out of others, first I must begin the journey to self-discovery.

I learn from myself to teach myself; learning what I can do and then going to do it, learning who I am and becoming Me. We all need assistance learning the intricate details about ourselves; we are what we say we are. If you only know a few good things about yourself but a lot of unpleasant details about you, then typically the unpleasant will be more frequently thought about just off the numbers. Looking deeper and deeper within reaching the point where I can toggle between objectivity and subjectivity, I have realized some interesting things which have helped me in forgiving.

Now I see why my dad would always say "once I found out what my [penis] was for that was it!". He was on his journey of self-discovery when he experienced sexual intercourse. It was so magnificent that he wanted more and more which is normal, but we must demonstrate physical restraint. With spiritual strength to fall back on in times of need, we must use our spirits to keep up on track. With not much to turn to but himself, he always did what he needed to live the life he desired.

Constantly looking to stay busy my dad wasn't left with a lot of time to focus on Self. Consistently caught up in what the world could offer him, I wonder if he ever thought about what he offered to the world. Succumbing to sexual desires prematurely, can derail your path because it can change everything completely as every thought must now be adjusted to accommodate more than previously expected.

Although sex is a form of creation and creativity, hence why the sacral chakra is located where it is, it should be done when you are established Spiritually, Mentally, and Physically, which is why marriage is suggested. Even in marriage good things can be abused if we are not healthy spiritually, mentally, and physically. When two individuals have grown to their peaks in health, they unite, reproduce, replenish, and continue the journey. We can have multiple peaks as well as the peak is relative to time, if you live right you will continue to rise. Living is accordance to what is right with your conscience is the key to health. Conscience isn't taught, its innate in each and every one of us.

I'm not exempt from anything. I also had to acknowledge my conscience more as I continue to develop as an adult. I understand as a young man, we come equipped with a sky-high libido. I innerstand and empathize with my dad as well during his experience with the same struggle of maintaining discipline. Only difference between my dad and I is that I'm more reserved, to the point where it manifests as shyness and nervousness around pretty women. I was socially awkward around any lady whom I wasn't accustomed to being around. Also, I wasn't into living risky primarily because of a woman.

Many of the girls I encountered, I was able manipulated with ease which became my enjoyment. I would see what I could get them to confess as a way to feed my ego. I didn't need to engage in sex to be satisfied. I was unable to give myself to anyone although my hunger for the action grew. Still very picky, I wouldn't engage with no others. Even after a break up, my libido never decreased so I had to pick up the slack somehow.

So, I resorted to watching adult films, igniting a new addiction. Could I have gone cold turkey? Who knows, but I wasn't willing to find out. I found myself creating a daily habit, sometimes two or three times. This starting at the typical age of adolescence years occurring alongside puberty

Although I never experienced sex at this point, I felt did in my mind. I say that to say, I'm no better than the next, only difference being the perception. Being reclusive made to turn inward for security versus outward to the world. I suppose it's the better route, certainly a safer route as there aren't as many dangers with your hands.

On the bright side I had a fun way to practice with my off hand, becoming ambidextrous, helping with multitasking. While under the veil of bodily urges it's a state of survival, relying on your animalistic half. What separates us from animals is our mind. Sex is indeed fun as we are sexual beings, but does that mean we lay down with everything walking? Not me, if I couldn't do it the right way I was fine alone. Once you drift in one area, you're liable to drift elsewhere.

I learned how to say no to others but never to myself. Now, I am learning to tell myself no and even admitting when I don't know. I don't know everything or even a lot of things but if it's interesting I'm willing to do research. Telling yourself *no* is true discipline but we don't think of it that way because we've heard no so much from others, we need some yeses in our life. So, we refrain from will and do whatever we want. A dangerous life to live as more enticing endeavors will find their way to you but will you be able to resist?

If one struggles to move beyond bodily urges then they are a child, spiritually. Through the spirit, we realize we are capable of much more. Then we realize that all we really need is discipline. An adult cannot discipline a child if they are the ones lacking discipline themselves. Discipline transcends the Natural Realm into the Supernatural. If you want to live Supernaturally then you must exude discipline. Discipline with health, wealth, and love.

The physical realm you occupy is a direct result of the mental and spiritual states you hold. We buy things for instant gratification for our work, but we'll constantly replace those things with new to keep that feeling of success all the while not actually being successful. Success doesn't fade unless you let it, or it was an illusion to begin with. Success is not contingent upon how much you possess either.

Many with many are empty inside because of over compensating outside to replace what they are missing inside. Fill your insides and you will not need for anything outside. Trust God in more instances than when you no longer know which move to make. Know that you are always with God through all steps and that guidance you long for will always be there. We always know of what's right, but we may not know which way to go. Tip: if it feels right, it is right. And know, whatever you do will be done to you.

The energy you give is what you manifest. Energy cannot be created because Energy is the Creator. Alpha and Omega, beginning and end, creation, and destruction; energy is only transformed. We are created from energy and decide our fate through our thoughts, words, and actions. What we think about becomes what we say which becomes what we do. The same is true when you substitute Thoughts for Feelings as they are dual opposites or complements.

Being steered by the spirit is an enlightening journey because you are being steered by the same energy which was used to create all there is. All that dwells within you is present only to ensure prosperity. If you believe in controlled chaos on one scale, don't you believe it to be true on all. The world is the way it is because one, we made it this way as humans, and two to test our Faith.

The world we live in tests our faith in God, in one another and ultimately in ourselves. The first part of the test is to realize that it is a test. Then as you survey the questions or begin to live you innerstand what you are being tested on. After time with the test, you realize why you are being tested in the first place. Tests show how much you know or to show what you should have learned thus far. With each test, you should have something different to work on. There's always somewhere to make improvements.

If you are missing questions to the test, then there's cause to pause. Ask yourself, have I learned from the previous opportunities? Am I still improving? Stagnation is the result of too much contentment in mediocrity. If you are okay with just being okay, then you aren't growing. When the environment you are placed in doesn't challenge you to grow to evolve, you won't improve. At this point you will have to accept the ultimate challenge of challenging yourself. It's cool to have someone who will push you to be great but if you aren't pushing yourself, you will never know what you're made of.

Only you know what you feel and what you feel is your potential to be the greatest. Sometimes we need others to reassure our confidence in ourselves because once we have security in ourselves, we naturally excel. Because of thoughts which were previously negative influencing our behavior, they are now positively based and serving us well. Challenges require you to experience what you can do. Some people know before others, some recognize in others, some recognize in the themselves. Once you begin to tap into *Pure Potentiality* you'll know no bounds as your language improves.

Language was simple

Language was simple
Names were complex
Today it is the opposite
We have the power to change what comes next
All I want to do
Show what it means to be True
Because I love you

Speak more positively
And you will gradually
Begin to see
How life is supposed to be
How to live naturally
How to master being free
How to balance masculine and femininity
Because we are all Energy
Just trust the Inner Me

Only release the affirmative version
Or you'll create a whirlwind
That you won't think will end
But you must know
That you are Good in the eyes of God
And that's how that go
Say that then
I AM Good
And allow God to live in
You, as you should

Language

Once upon a time, *nigga* was my favorite term to use. Even knowing the history didn't stop me from using it because I figured, like many today, we can flip a negative into a positive. This is a partial truth; although our intention may be respectful, at the end of the day it still means ignorant. So, we are speaking ignorance into existence each time we utter the term. This was a profound revelation I received one night providing an explanation of why to continuously monitor speech.

As you look around at the state of the world, there is an immense amount of ignorance, countless individuals purposely avoiding the Truth. No matter how much access we get to the truth or how many expose the truth, people simply don't pay attention. Elimination of *this* term from my vocabulary is imperative for this very reason. I now choose to inspire, and rather than continue a cycle, I am breaking the cycle, severing the cycle.

All that is comes from all that *is*, and it only makes sense. For my people that are getting plenty of money I say to you, "yeah you're getting money but who has more cents?". Spend your money to make positive change. Since you always have the power to grow, as growth is change, become eternal. Just because you change doesn't mean you've grown; people switch up all the time, going from annoying behavior to disturbing behavior to alarming. Consistent growth is about recognizing weaknesses, accepting them, and ushering in a new era. Accept who you are to become all that you are meant to be, One, where all you possess is strengths.

During growth, we recognize that whatever is said is being released into the Universe, no matter the intent. Saying what you do *not* want is leaving the possibility for it to manifest because it was said. Whatever you say is what *is* because we create our reality through our words and thoughts. Thinking unpleasantly will affect your mood changing what you are attracting by manipulating your Energy signal. If we are not conscious of our Frequency any reality is liable to be created or worse, but we must rise.

Consciously release Love, a high frequency to vibrate in, attracting positivity because darkness is always lurking. Whether you are in a positive or negative space you'll be tested. The first test is to see what you're liable to say, then to see how polarized your emotions are, and finally which emotions will you act on. Everything can always be better only you must understand what's Good. In understanding good you'll know how to manifest more good. Good and good is better, keep compounding more good and you'll see better and do better. Love leads to better and better leads to more love, it's a good cycle.

Unfortunately, we cannot change the purpose of something after it has been created, it will always mean what it originally meant. After God has created, layers can be added to the purpose, but the essence remains the same, so when you speak, always speak in the affirmative. Using 'not' does not negate the action that follows; you are speaking into existence whatever you release from your mouth. Watch closely for verbs that have been altered to include a negating prefix, this does not nullify the fact that you spoke negativity into the atmosphere. Creation does not change; the environment simply adds a new layer. We must remember to seek the true purpose to innerstand how it is to be utilized to achieve the goal.

If you are like me, a work in progress, start by replacing negative terms with affirmative ones only speaking what you intend to say. Align your speech with your intentions, innerstand the art of articulation to create the reality you feel should exist. Energy can only be transformed so transform the dark energy into light energy by speaking blessings over yourself, your life and all those present.

We even need to bless those whose presence isn't deserving a blessing, nonetheless everyone is deserving of a blessing. God blesses those who deserve blessing, you house God so bless those who surround you to reach new heights and bless more people continuing the cycle. You do this until those whom you have blessed are blessing others and creating their own cycle.

Because I am a conscious creator, I must think about everything I say in depth. To learn to say a word is one thing, to know the definition is another, but how a word is *spelled* is the game. They want to turn you away from your original culture, especially with the English language. They want to see allegiance and an investment of time to adopt the English language as your own shows them just that.

Words such as: phone, light, brought, receipt, aisle, etc. do not fit the mold of being able to sound them out. These are terms we must simply know how to spell but defy the norms. Words are spells, and thinking of everything you release as a spell will create a cautious being in you. Knowing the magnitude of the words you say will lead you tailoring your life.

In America, wherever you travel there is a Sun people community you'll also notice there is a dialect that only they speak. Where else do we experience various forms of the same language? Africa; we are not meant to speak the English language as it was created to dumb us down linguistically. We must return to our roots and abandon our imitative ways. Why do you think so many say you are speaking *white* when you speak proper English? Your own look at you as a sellout for succumbing to the "American" way or Ice people's way.

Hearing others speak, knowing what I know now, it's disturbing how possessive their speech is, majority of what we say is ours is not; the game is so deep. So many times, I hear "me, my, mine" in instances where what you consider to be yours is an illusion. My car, my house, my store, my my my; you make payments on your car so it's really the bank's car, same with your house and the store you represent belongs to the company. Many companies instill this possessiveness into their employees to give them a sense of responsibility but in turn leaves the employee stressed and the company reaps the harvests.

Be very mindful of your speech and realize that not much, if any, is truly ours. Only that which we create is ours and even then, it's for the people otherwise it wouldn't have been created. Our perceptions need expansion to include more than just ourselves, this is such selfish behavior. Yes, you matter but you are no different from the one next to you. People simply want recognition, which isn't a bad thing, but the lengths we go to is the issue. If you are deserving, you will be acknowledged and receive *your* blessing.

More speech to be corrected; saying "I forgot" is putting the blame on memory pretending you have no control over maintaining a thought. Be completely honest and admit you simply weren't thinking about it. If you cannot be honest with yourself who can you be honest with. And if you can be honest with yourself you can be honest with anybody.

The most important part in voicing, is honesty, as the Truth is God's message, so tell the truth. Many people only focus on the truth within holy books and that's the only truth they know. Many only tell of the truth they've seen with the natural eyes. For instance, if you go to college you will make more money. That is a true statement, but it is conditional, and the same goes for natural eyes truth, it's not the whole story told.

The truth is typically associated with religion but if one is not responding to "religious truths" move to a different subject. There are more ways to reveal truth versus only teaching that which came directly from a Holy book. Many people today don't live all of which is present, they haven't even learned it to apply it, yet teach from it. Practice what you preach, and your life will change. Tell good, do good, be good. Do right, be right, live right. Love life, love to live, live to love. Preach about what you practice. Talk about the Good you perform to inspire more good. Talking about good will bring about more good to fruition.

Words are magic. I've learned that abracadabra, a term used by many magicians, means *I create as I speak* in Hebrew. Words can't be seen yet they can be felt because they are the bridge between the unseen and seen. They are vibrational frequencies which manipulate the material realm. We create materials in this realm with our hands but the intangibles like events, realities, and occurrences are created by thoughts, feelings, words, and actions.

I watched a documentary which revealed that in the original languages, if spoken correctly, will shift *sand* into the shape of letters. Quite literally our original alphabets were created by speaking and recording what was said. The English language was created to instill a disconnect between the hemispheres of the brain between thought and feeling. Words are a mental/spiritual realm, depending on the language, frequency exuded through the body.

The body is the weakest aspect of You. Many are judged by others based upon their body's performance. The body goes as the Mind leads as the spirit guides. The mind is where choice lies and where conscience lies. Conscience is also present in the heart because the heart and brain are cornerstones in the body. Thinking and Feeling.

Thoughts are either generated in the mind or received in the mind in the form or revelation from the spirit. So, we either send thought to the spirit realm to be magnified or simply receive what's given. Words come from within to create what we feel/think. Be very mindful of this uniqueness to us as it is very sensitive whether you personally feel you are sensitive or not. We asked to steer the ship so now we should come through on our end.

A job and work are not the same thing. A career isn't always work either, but they are typically more promising than jobs only because of more money and more security. Work is the productive action you naturally perform. A career is just a guaranteed pay rate no matter the number of hours worked. Work is progressive and fulfilling to you and those surrounding you, it is purposeful.

Which is why I decided to end my college career after three and a half semesters, my definition of work changed drastically. I knew after studying the Bible for a month that corporate America was not where I belonged, doing taxes, and managing companies' finances is not what I am here to do. Throughout my high school career, I was associating what I was good at, math, with the job I was seeking. These days I understand that math isn't the only thing I am good at but during those days it was my haven because everything was more literal and less biased.

So today I know for sure that I want to be a farmer because we all go to work for food, but we can simply grow our own food. The food we buy is not fueling us and it is by design. Those in power feel we have reached a point where depopulation is the only answer to the changes earth is experiencing because depopulation will make their job of controlling the planet easier.

Growing your own food is the way to go as you can manage what is entering and leaving your body. In the beginning that was Man's first working place, in the garden ensuring he and his family were well fed. We are paying for things that are naturally free, well not truly free but do not require money to acquire. Growing food is an investment of time and during this time our connection to Earth will grow tremendously as you must understand all Her cycles and when to plant what.

Remember, we are to guard our tongues because the very words we utter shape the material realm. Formulate your own thoughts without influence of the world around you because the world is wicked. Much of what you see on television and even the internet is filtered to be negative to sway your thoughts. Understanding the ulterior motives of the *elite* or people with more money than they can spend, will lead you to recognizing the depth of the trickery. Your tongue is the double-edged sword the Bible speaks about because you have the power to speak life or death into anything. This includes yourself and whatever you encounter along your journey.

Be careful with idioms as well as they are literal to the subconscious and the universe. I would give examples but I'm not speaking up any negativity for the sake of making a point, so you will just have to use your imagination. Anything you say is being released into the atmosphere to be a potential reality, we must think on this level if we are to change the course of our future. Take your words very seriously, joking is fine but at what length are you willing to go to for a laugh. Laughter is a part of happiness and bliss but remember to leave it in the Light where it is beneficial to all.

Some say we should "think before we speak" but I challenge the belief as I begin to understand the true power of words. I feel we are to think before, during, and after speaking to consciously sustain our lives. Thinking before will present the opportunity of tailoring your words to best suit the situation at hand. Thinking during speech is your chance to listen to yourself and learn from yourself. Thinking after you have said what you intended to say will strengthen your ability to assess your language to determine if was appropriate.

Language is a way to either express Love or Fear, whether your words are positive or negative will determine which you are expressing. Expression is through the throat chakra or Vishuddha which is influenced by the Heart and Third Eye chakras. Your thoughts and feelings flow from your throat into the atmosphere to create either what you feel or think. We determine which we feed energy to, and whatever you feed will have life. Some say that fear is an illusion and I agree partially. Although fear is not real, it still is. Even if one masters their fears, that doesn't eliminate fear completely, just from a single host.

Before the fall of Man, we didn't know of fear. It wasn't until after he took a bite of the apple from the Tree of Knowledge of Good and Evil that he seen the whole perspective. Knowledge is indeed power, but we should know everything we see isn't always what is. There's always an opposite that exists, polarity is a universal law; as so above, so below. Sure, you can say we are supposed to know of fear but being that we do, there's reasoning behind it. Do I know for certain what that reason is? Definitely not, but I do see that fear is necessary.

Everyone's learning curve is different, so it takes a different amount of fear for anyone to grasp a concept and move to the next. Fear either drives one into Love or into more fear. The moment you step out of fear, you step into Love. Many have said this, and this also lets me know Love/Fear are two halves of the same whole. Everything has positive and negative aspects, so if we are to take the bad with the good, we must at least innerstand what *bad* truly is and it isn't bad.

Use the language of two more realms in their union to reveal more truth. Though the language of religion and science differ, we find they tell the same story. In some instances, they refer to the same occurrence in others they reference a sequence of events. The languages begin merging to tell a complete truth but only once the foundation has been settled. Though many in their respective realms seem to vehemently disagree with one another, they are really in competition to see who tells the better stories. Comprehension is a key concept in this game called *life*.

How

How do you go from
A hangnail to a broken thumb
Living the life to becoming a bum
Mismanagement is the answer to this one
Take care of needs first
Or did you not think the bubble would eventually burst
But I bet you make the tires "skurt"
Might as well write *clown* on your shirt
Cause you are a goofy
Need to be in a hoopty
To instill humility

Be more humble
Cause you ain't ready for a rumble
With nature
Which includes the cosmos
I know you're wondering
How do I know
I always know who's willing to grow
I see it in the eyes
Who really tries

Dig deeper
Trying is dying
You wanna meet the reaper
Or you wanna keep flying
Soar high
Even beyond the sky
Into space
And experience eternal grace

Completion

Everything was created to be perfect forever with evolution as the goal; but the question remains, how do we evolve into God? I read a story once, actually more than once, about an atheist guy meeting God. The story blew my mind, not because he met God but because all his questions were answered. Being that he was an atheist you know he had some awesome questions to ask as he doesn't believe in God period. In this story, *God* revealed that He is purely a natural phenomenon which simply evolved into being.

Now I don't know how true this story is as some believe it is satirical but enough was said for me to consider the possibility. Let alone all the questions asked were answered with such directness and sometimes being a bit vague but honest as The Most High does in conversation with me. As I digress, shall we return to evolution?

Expand your consciousness and grow into a more advanced being. Let go of worldly possessions as they lose relevancy as most if not all are not required to sustain life. Look deep within to understand who you are and what you need in order to thrive. Currently we are in the survival state of life, but we must transcend into thriving. Bypass the "middle man", that is, societal norms which do not dictate your existence although it may appear so at times. As you tap into Self and continue to transform, unify with your brothers and sisters. Unify as you share knowledge to improve the rate at which we evolve.

We shall be One as we are all humans and work together with each other's best interest. Competition between ranks can be healthy but not at the expense of loss of life. "Maximize pleasure and minimize pain", is what

God said in the conversation the guy had. That's what He referred to as the purpose for Life and evolution. Do not make life more difficult than it already is by thinking of your family as your enemies.

Also, we must lose the need to be in control, as one group of humans does not possess the aptitude to determine what is best for all of us. Lose the ego and focus more on your spiritual self. Locking into the spirit self you can harness the energy you have always had all along. Use this energy to spread Love as we progress to the next level. Loving your neighbor will inspire and empower them to do the same while accepting differences.

Everyone is different for a reason, that reason being we are to accomplish different tasks. We all have unique abilities, so just as Man and Woman become One, so will we as we unite as a species. In unison, we fill all gaps like water, respecting and loving one another for we rely upon one another for the security of our home, Earth.

Science and religion should learn from each other, that's why they both exist; to tell their perspective. Without either you are missing some of the Truth, we need all the information to complete the Word. There are things that cannot be explained but were discovered in which case Science has access to. Religion needs these things but are too stern on using modified texts to prove their point running solely on belief rather than know.

Religion needs to learn to use information to their advantage and compound wisdom by applying what they read to experience science. Science's view is dim because they want distinct communication about discoveries. They focus on proof to others, but they don't understand that you will never know if someone truly believes you. Science is missing something, ways to explain phenomenon. Science is one to observe but rarely speaks of the existence of God as if that's not our Source.

To complete the picture, we must align Religious truths with Scientific truths. They clash as of now because of the way the story of the Truth is told. Religion is more so based from belief versus knowledge. Let's start by understanding that many, if not all, religions were created during the Age of Pisces or the Age of Belief. Science is objective, while religion is subjective.

Religions are subjective because no one would know of their existence as they are based on perspectives of the way of Life. The differences between religions causes friction when their sources would suggest otherwise. The Torah, Bible, and Qur'an are composed of very similar messages on how to carry yourself in this realm. But when you look out into the world they don't seem to have knowledge of each other, so they act out in fear rather than embracing each other.

The different Holy Books represent different languages over the world. The Torah is originally written in Hebrew along with the Bible which was eventually translated into English by King James who was said to be a lot of things. Continuing the subject, the Qur'an was originally in Arabic, but if all are read in your native language you'll see how similar the messages are.

Contrary to popular belief, religion and science are one in the same but separated to further confuse the commoner. If religion is a fairytale, science is the actual factual that validates what's said. They are to be studied in unison to fully grasp the concepts.

The Torah is simply the first five books of the Bible; Genesis, Exodus, Leviticus, Numbers, and Deuteronomy. The Bible goes on to include books from prophets and include a New Testament which focuses on The Son of God and His teachings. The Qur'an has books on many of the main people mentioned in the Bible, i.e. Abraham, Moses, Joseph, Mary, Jesus, David, Solomon, the list goes on.

Only difference being the Qur'an includes the Prophet Muhammad, who isn't mentioned in either of the other works. I've read that Muhammad learned about the Bible first before writing the Qur'an, which is the reason they are so similar. I've seen that the Bible was heavily rooted in Ancient Kemetic/Egyptian teachings. I've even seen that the first Bible was written on papyrus which comes from Egypt originally.

My perspective is that if there are so many works say the same thing shouldn't we be more eager to receive the message. At this point it doesn't matter which came first as time is not linear, only our perception of time is. Until you receive the message you will remain in this clashing phase of Life.

"As so above, so below" is one of seven Hermetic principles. Three of our chakras are above, the Throat, Third Eye, and Crown. The throat is your method of communication to materialize what you envision in your Third Eye coming from the influential cosmic energy flowing through your crown chakra.

The Three below are the Solar Plexus, Sacral and Root. Your strength coming from your belly to create what you are passionate about in the sacral but remaining connected to Earth as She is your foundation to remind you of all you are. In the center of these six is the is the seventh, Heart chakra which is where Life began for you.

Operating in your lower frequencies, your revelation will reflect your evolution as a human. Functioning solely in your animalistic ways will leave you fighting for survival not realizing everyone can survive and thrive. Raising your vibration allows you to tap into God within you.

Your beating heart was your first sign of life, your original rhythm in sync with the vibrations surrounding you. Your heart center is where the two halves of you are united to become God, your heart is your connection to God. A hardened heart doesn't receive love nor let it flow within, a softened heart allows for our original frequency to flow freely throughout the vessel we occupy.

In the Earth, Life goes as we go because we have dominion here. Not to say we are rulers, but we have an inherent obligation to ensure Life continues. We are the only animal combined with God by virtue of a Spirit, we as in humanoids. I say humanoids because humans aren't the only being that exists. It's irrational to think humans are the only intelligent communicative species of humanoid to live.

There are others out there and even others on and within Earth. There's much more to be discussed but we must explore more and ask more questions. Exploring more connects you with Earth and thus the Cosmic realm leading you away from your lower frequencies. This leaves you confident to receive powerful revelation knowing you can act on what you have seen.

God is everything within everything, Energy, whom communicates as we do, through vibrational frequencies. Sound is a vibrational frequency tuned to the ear. If the tone is strong enough it can be physically felt throughout the entire body. Objects that we can see are tuned to a different frequency as well as smell. If we have a tool to manipulate frequency, then we can change anything. Think of a microwave, all it does is emit a very high frequency focused on whatever is twirling on the plate to change the frequency of the object.

Water provides excellent examples of how a change in frequency results in a change in matter. A gentleman by the name of Dr. Masaru Emoto, studied the effects of words on water. In his experiments, he would observe crystals of frozen water after showing letters to water, showing pictures to water, playing music to water, and praying to water. The results are astounding. The hexagonal shaped crystals would either look beautiful or distorted based upon the experience of the water. I wish they taught about these studies in public school systems, the kids would be amazed as would their parents when they returned home to share what they learned.

By this point you should have made the connection between spoken word, frequency, and water or the human body. Also, aside from spoken word, pictures represent words which we will discuss in the next chapter. If water can be affected by frequency, wouldn't the body as well which is more water than anything else. The biochemistry of humans needs to be assessed and addressed on a mass scale.

As I spoke of Dr. Sebi previously, he studied biochemistry and realized that all illnesses were due to mucus build up in certain places. Because if this discovery he cured individuals of cancers, herpes, HIV, AIDS, etc. many of which considered incurable by traditional doctors. The main thing he did was change his patients' diet to plant-based then feed them from a cellular level.

On the other hand, much of the pharmaceutical industry provides medication which doesn't cure a thing. Pharmaceuticals only suppress the side effects inducing more side effects which require more medication. Let's also establish a fact that much of medication today is oil based. This is because there are individuals that are heavily invested in oil and to capitalize on their investments, oil must be a commodity.

Also, I have learned that doctors aren't even trained on nutrition which is incredible seeing as their sole purpose is to *heal* people. They simply know how to treat side effects and it hasn't been about curing for some time now. The cycle is genius in terms of profit but morally sinister not to help individuals become healthier especially because they claim to do so. They leave a lot of valuable information out of the picture so well that the average person doesn't realize they have been duped.

No one tells you that chakras, the energy centers we learned about earlier correspond to the endocrine system which is made up of various glands throughout the body.

Also known as the hormone system they are found in all mammals, birds, fish, and many other living organisms. Hormones regulate insulin or blood sugar, growth, function of reproductive organs and energy production. We have the pituitary and pineal gland in the place of the Crown and Third Eye chakra. The thyroid gland with the Throat chakra, thymus with the heart chakra, pancreas and adrenal gland corresponding with the solar plexus chakra. The ovaries and testes correspond with the sacral chakra and root chakra.

God is also present in the form of laminin, a cross-shaped enzyme that holds protein together. This protein at the basis of all human beings to facilitate life. Ironic how often we discover clues that point to a divine creator. Learning of all the synchronicities and alignments that must ensue for us to even live screams of an intelligent parent.

All I ever wonder is who else knows this information and what are they doing with it. I don't see many talk about laminin but I'm not sure where to look. I know for sure we were not briefed on the importance of laminin in grade school and I can understand it because of the religious tie seeing as they removed all religion affiliation from school. There's so much we don't question that needs to be questioned if we are to ever learn.

Have you or anyone you know asked their doctor for their child's umbilical cord? Were they given a hard time about it? That's because they know something, and we can all feel it or some even know. We know that our DNA will heal our DNA. In the medical industry, because everything is a business first today, they use umbilical cords to extract stem cells. These stem cells come through the umbilical cord from the placenta. Stem cells heal anything, and it only makes sense that our bodies come equipped to heal ailments. On several levels, we are shown how we are the problem and solution.

All life can heal on its own on some level and if on some level it's on all levels. All life comes from water and water is influenced by words. Furthermore, water is a representation of how Energy affects it because frequencies can change the properties of water. For instance, the oil spill in the Gulf of Mexico a few years ago. Scientists played frequencies while on the water to cure it, removing the oil which brought the animal life back. Another example of frequencies and water is through Dr. Emoto. Dr. Masaru Emoto studied the effects of words and sounds on water. Positive words or phrases resulted in beautiful hexagonal snowflakes while negative phrases formed distorted figures. The beautiful creations were symmetrical and showed me a new way to become whole.

Epigenetics says once the environment changes the health state of the cells change. A cells environment is equivalent to your aura or etheric field of energy surrounding you. The better the energy you receive the better you begin to feel. As you begin to speak more positively your natural vibration will speed up. This means that your Frequency is getting higher and higher allowing you to realize that you come prepackaged as a Self-healer.

Another way of becoming whole comes in the form of epigenetics. Epigenetics is changing a cell's environment versus altering the cell. To go deeper, epigenetics takes away our ability to blame any misfortunes in our body on our parents' genetic make-up. Typically, when faced with a problem, humans today would adjust the wrong aspect. Adjusting the environment points to a larger issue of our environment and the impact it has on us. This knowledge comes has been around but really becoming more prevalent in the Age of Aquarius.

As mentioned before, many religions were born in the Age of Belief well today we are in the Age of Know or Age of Aquarius. Notice how popular the internet is today, and how accessible information is, today is also referred to as the Information Age. The Age of Pisces ended on Dec. 21, 2012, this was also the significant day many thought the world would end.

It marked the beginning of the end as an incredible shift would be made in the consciousness of the masses. Many are now more interested in learning of the true ways of the world and thus pray for it to end. Please note that the world ending has nothing to do with Earth ending. Earth will continue to live as we devise new ways to reconnect ourselves to Her versus what we have created in the world.

Spiritually led by darkness the masses are waking up to realize they do not want the life they are living they want to live better and in harmony. We all know things are not in the best condition, but we don't see how we can be impactful. I promise you this piece of literature will help you on your journey to righteousness. Seek and you will discover, ask and you shall receive. These are karmic laws that we must recognize as such because we are creating a realm of destruction unconsciously. Become conscious again because all is cyclical, so we are to elevate our level of thinking.

Intuition is associated with the right hemisphere of the brain while the left side with thought. As a Pisces, there's a natural duality to be innerstood. Intuition is guidance from universal forces, thought of as God. Faith is knowing the Energy leading you is leading you to prosperity. Faith is following your intuition which is God guidance or guidance coming from The All Eternal.

Pisces are to find and recognize the balances of Life. We see everything from multiple perspectives which is why we are tasked with Understanding. Pisces encompass traits from all other eleven zodiac signs giving us the ability to relate to everyone thus understand everyone. Astrology is the study of the stars and planetary alignment; these aspects of the solar system play a part in who we are as beings.

The left brain is associated with logic, thought, and reasoning. Western philosophies are heavily rooted in left brain mentalities. For instance, the importance of money is analytical, sure it can provide for a better life in some regard but one's perspective will remain incomplete putting money first.

Honestly, money is not a necessity to live but given the current influences money is made to be perceived as such. This only puts a select few in power and keeps them with much of the power to change. Incorporate more right brain or Eastern Philosophies to balance your Ego driven life. Thought comes from us and thus Ego, balance the Ego with the Higher Self to *be* all You are.

You are the way you are partially because of where you are, Spiritually, Mentally, and Physically. Also because of your name, birthdate, and birth time. Time determines who we are to be. The specific time you were born begins your foundation. The date, day, month, year, hour, minute, even second and so forth, all play a part in who you are.

I learned of the meaning behind being born on a Waxing Gibbous Moon, the phase right before a full moon. "You like to question things and have issues settled before going to work on a problem. You appreciate art, elegant forms, and efficient designs. You seek deep meanings in things that you see and want your actions to make the world a better place." Consider all things unique to you to receive more of an explanation as to why you are the way you are.

Be sure to look in to the numbers also, they give great insight to provide more perspective on the sides of you that you haven't began to explore. The numbers surrounding you tell you your story and give you access to You. Learn more about Self to better consciously combat anything you encounter. Know that you have the power to change and change i. Always simplify and work smarter.

4

Fo'
Where do I go
Who shall I take
What is a break
Is it the brakes
Or is it a break
Break like a vacay
Are you tryna get paid
How you gonna stay safe
Keep ya founday straight
How you do that tho
You gotta balance ya soul
Now what in the world does that mean
You gotta have your own dream
You gotta dream to be King, or Queen
But you know they got slaves
And even if they don't
You really think their "servants" gettin' paid
Cause they just spendin' they days
Doing whatever they say
But I can't live it that way
Nah I can't live it that way

88i8

Forever is infinity
I AM forever
Life is forever
I can remember
I can deliver
Whatever's needed
To stop the bleedin'
Cause we conceited
For whatever reason
All I can see is
Where I'm s'pose to be n
How I'm s'pose to keep it
What I'm s'pose to do n
When I'm gonna reap it

4ever

I have always had a knack for numbers, as math was my favorite subject growing up and I loved to gamble at family gatherings. Great at playing cards, I wanted to use my gift to get what I wanted, more materials but more so to display my level of understanding concepts. We'd play Black Jack, Tonk, and Gin Rummy with me typically winning.

Many my age struggled in the very subject I excelled at with ease. I didn't have to think outside the box in math, everything was straight to the point; add, subtract, multiply, and divide. Learn the concept of what is happening and apply it.

My attraction to numbers led me to believe I wanted to be a CFO in high school. Nothing wrong with being the financial head of a company but nowadays I question corporate America's interest in the well-being of

Earth. I don't see much of a connection but then again, I am not looking for one neither.

In middle school, when it was time to start thinking about college/careers, I had no clue what to search. I was thinking veterinarian because I liked animals and would deal well in rehabilitation then I saw the education requirements, followed by the realization that large animal vets on average made less than those that dealt with smaller animals. So I sought a switch, over hearing a good friend of mine at the time was considering accounting because he was good with numbers, I thought, hey me too, I could also be an accountant.

So, throughout high school I would lean on my understanding of numbers to know just how much I needed to do to keep my B average. Rarely doing homework at home, if it couldn't be mostly completed in class it wouldn't have gotten completed. I strategically took L's because I knew what I could afford.

The older I got, the more strategic I got, learning what I needed to graduate, not seeking the most challenging route. Why would I do that? I didn't care about accolades nor felt the need to prove to anyone I could get straight A's. I knew then that good grades weren't a reflection of intellect, but a reflection of obedience and memory. I did minimal, 30% of the homework, did all class work and skated through.

By senior year I was taking two marketing courses and two office aide periods, that's over half the schedule comprised of easy A's. Grade school wasn't the challenge it was made out to be and once I knew that occasional C's were acceptable, I really started chilling. The chilling created a habit of laziness and procrastination and at 23 I began to leave that phase of Life. Having jobs helps with that because you can perceive money as your reason for moving but money should never be your main focus. It takes a renewal of the Spirit to cleanse the Mind which facilitates through the Body. This leads you to discovering your purpose, which always incorporates your knack, whatever it may be. Purpose is the ignition to your passion, the flame that burns within.

Also, in senior year I was taking two AP courses, Calculus, and Literature, mainly because of the teachers. I understood some of the Calculus, about forty percent, but Mr. Kasumba always said even if we didn't do well in the course, we'd be better off in college because we were familiar with the material. After devoting a bit of effort, I quickly realized it'd take much more effort than I was willing to dedicate, so I shot for a cool C which would average as a B towards my GPA.

In Literature, Ms. Silveri's class, Room 110, was where I first received the freedom to explore. A free period some days, we would sit, think, and have group discussions about Life. If I was the Me now, I would go back to be a part of a discussion to raise the level of our thinking even more. It was high then but imagine if the kids in high school grasped this wisdom coming to you in this book. Perhaps, I still can make a difference in the lives of those who are learning.

A long digression of my school life to lead back into my "dream" of being an accountant at the top, a CFO. This was the time where that idea came originated. At the time, I was simply saying what I knew could make sense, but I saw none of it in my future. At that time, I couldn't see past tomorrow. I couldn't even imagine being twenty-one at seventeen and eighteen. I was solely cerebral, no intuition was developed at that time, I didn't know what I was going to do. I only knew I was taking a path separate from my older brother, one more "safe".

I thought I was going to Kennesaw State to major in Finance, minor in Spanish, live on campus, and pledge Kappa Alpha Psi. I did get into KSU even though I had to take a placement test because my ACT scores were decent at best. I performed outstanding on the required test but sad to say I never lived that "dream". I couldn't afford it and FAFSA is only cool if your parents cooperate with the process, it took two years to finally complete everything needed to attend college.

By this time my ideology was beginning to shift, I was now attending the local Clayton State, majoring in Accounting because Finance wasn't available but still minoring in Spanish. On my first day of Intro to University, my professor asks, "why do people go to college?". He let a few students answer, and the typical answers used were "education", "to get out the house" but none of which were the most correct. He said people go to college to make more money. And when that began to marinate my ideology of college began to shift.

No longer was I striving to achieve my goal of Summa Cum Laude, just to make more money. The same more money I'd make if I graduated with a 3.2. Making more money doesn't require we live like college students; broke and ignorant. They keep you in the classroom and give your just enough money to pay to be there. The stress isn't worth it to me and when I realized I could be much more effective without the institution, my life changed for the better. It only took three and a half semesters before knowing that wasn't where I needed to be. I did however learn how to research and have one of my English professors compliment my writing style.

With me reading the Bible for myself I realized what work truly is and I didn't need college to work. But college can be useful to you if you are learning what you wish, something valuable to Earth. While in college, I finally learned why I am alive which led me to what it means to be alive and how I carry out my purpose for living.

During the time, I was attending college, I also had a girlfriend. Looking back that was a time for us to get to know ourselves individually and prosper. Although, had we learned ourselves instead of each other there'd be a void waiting to be filled. Even with us teaching each other and later learning ourselves still left a void to be filled in me. Our moment together caused a slight delay in our progression but to be twenty-four with no attachment to the world, I can go wherever I want.

It may seem like a delay, but two years is better than 18, and Lord knows it could've well been the case. I thank God every day everything happening just the way it did. I am still young and I still have opportunity with access to the Unlimited. Energy is abundant and for all of us to use, aren't you here? Then it's on purpose; use what you need to do what you do for All.

Also during this time, I got my first glimpse into Numerology, I was told by a coworker to consider my Life Path Number as it would reveal my purpose. Well my number is One and it's for born leaders which is interesting because I was always following someone else's lead. Took me a couple of years to fully delve into Numerology but I was already beginning to carry myself differently.

Upon leaving college, I purchased my full Numerology report and had my Mind blown. My interest in numbers brought me here, realizing the numbers surrounding us tell a story. I read a book on me not written by me, that was based on an algorithm, safe to say I was creeped out at the accuracy. Now much of my characteristics I didn't know, in the sense the words used to expound were new to me.

Aware of how I felt and learning the words to pair to feelings is how we begin to connect more strands. Uniting the left brain with and the right brain with meaning behind the numbers. Giving you more positive descriptive words to describe yourself so you can thank yourself in a positive manner, which is the key to success, speech.

In numerology, the study of numbers, each number one through nine means something different. Numerology taught me how to conquer me. During this process, I learned more about myself in a matter of weeks than I did my entire life. After purchasing my complete numerology report via Numerologists.com which was over 200 pages, I began to read.

The depth of the knowledge of me was immense and the weirdest part was the fact that I was named before being born. Our name is one of the first things we are identified by. Never in my wildest dreams would I imagine how profound my name was. Not only that but the significance of my birthdate which reveals the Life Path number.

To learn more about yourself I highly recommend using numerology as a resource. It gives you tons of insight into who you are based on your full name and birthdate. Based on your name you are shown what it equates to because each letter of the alphabet corresponds to a single digit number.

In my case, Khadeem Jibreel Thomas equates to 11-7-22. These numbers are highly important as they determine the type of person you are and how to conquer the weaknesses you claim. 11 is the most intuitive number, 7 is the philosopher's number and 22 is a master builder's number. What numbers make up who you are?

It's even more interesting to see how the numbers align with the given meaning of my name. Let's start with Khadeem, which means servant of God, corresponding with eleven a master number for intuition. Eleven is the most intuitive number showing in more than one way that I am to be in tune with the Higher Power.

The way you get eleven is to take the value of each letter 2+8+1+4+5+5+4 = 29 2+9 = 11. To find the values of the alphabet, start by writing out the numbers one through nine. Following this, start writing out the alphabet under the numbers, upon reaching nine begin again at one until you finish at 'z'.

As far is Jibreel, my middle name, which according to my mom, randomly came to her first cousin as she blurted out 'Jibreel'. Jibreel is the Arabic form of Gabriel which means God is my strength. Also, we should familiarize ourselves with the Angels, doing so we'd know of Archangel Gabriel who is God's messenger.

This all plays a role when we discover the numerical value for Jibreel is seven. Seven is the philosopher's number, philosophers are known to be intricate thinkers and speakers, giving, and receiving deep messages. Philosophers exist to understand and explain the complexities of Life in a simplified manner. Seven is also seen as a number of perfection in the Bible.

Lastly, we have Thomas, meaning twin which ironically equates to twenty-two. Twenty-two is a master number, more specifically Master Builder. Individuals with the number twenty-two can materialize their dreams.

Thomas is also the name of one of Jesus' Disciples. He was the disciple that didn't believe Jesus was resurrected and needed proof of His wounds suffered on the cross. This provides me with the explanation that I have an intense drive to receive confirmation before I accept knowledge. Numbers help to paint the picture that is, me.

In Indian Numerology, my name receives more perspective to further complete myself. We begin with Khadeem, corresponding to 2, meaning teacher. Associated with the moon, 2 is feminine in nature, also keep in mind that women are the teachers of households. We move on to Jibreel equating to 1, symbolizing leader, in conjunction with the sun and Sunday, the first day of the week. Quick side note, I do not know how they calculate their numbers, I retrieved mine through a website. Lastly, we have Thomas, totaling to 9, meaning humanist and aligned with planet Mars.

In addition to the numbers, I am also provided with Karmic lessons for each of my names. Khadeem with the lesson of individual stability, corresponding to 11, my numerical value through traditional numerology, as the most intuitive. We go on to Jibreel, with the lesson of renunciation, corresponding to the 7, meaning philosopher also embracing my spiritual enlightenment. Then we have Thomas with the lesson of patience, which is a necessity of the Master Builder I embody from the 22 my last name reduces to. Remember to study the core of you first which will lead you to the rest of you.

"If you only knew the magnificence of the 3, 6 and 9, then you would have a key to the universe." – Nikola Tesla.

9 is one if the more interesting numbers as it is the last single digit. Nine is shaped such that from within everything is created and it resembles the Fibonacci spiral.

Also with nine it can be added to any number only to be summed to that very number that was added to it. For example, if you add nine and five the result is fourteen but one and four add to five. Always reduce multiple digits to their single form. Nine is nothing and everything simultaneously. Another example of this is if you add the numbers one through eight, the reduced result is nine. Even when you include nine the result remains the same.

Remember, trinity is the basis; such that three are *one* and make up everything, nine. Six, however, is your connection; it is a representation of humans, the created, and where we reside in the grand scheme. Shaped as an inward spiral in on itself, it's a reflection of either Love **or** Fear. You are God's creation, the six, from everything to the slightest thing returning to the center to finish.

With Love, the Heart center, we became Life. But if you hold fear in your heart, you create darker realities we must overcome. Out of Love came Life, our chance to share an experience and the Frequency of the moment is 528Hz. Look into vortex mathematics to get a deeper understanding of the significance of three, six and nine.

We do have visual guides present in the universe only we must first be knowledgeable about them and then learn how to recognize them. Angel numbers are a form, whereas the numbers we find ourselves encountering is really a message from the angels surrounding you. Everyone is assigned an angel or multiple angels to guide them throughout life and numbers is their way of communicating with you.

Sure, you might ask why not just talk to me, why make it more difficult, but numbers came before letters as numbers are universal. There are different websites you may explore that will explain to you what each set of numbers mean. How can it be trusted? Try it out and see if you want it to apply or not. I've looked into several sets of numbers to see their meaning and it was surely what I needed to continue my journey.

I'll provide a couple of examples of numbers which have been reoccurring and their meaning. '221' "The more you can stay positive (in your thoughts, speech, actions, and written words), the better this experience will be for you and your loved ones". '143' "There's no need to worry, the ascended masters and angels are right by your side, assuring you a positive outcome".

Whenever I see 221 in random places, I am reminded to remain positive with my thoughts, words, and actions. Seeing certain numbers repeatedly is, to me, a gentle reminder of the goals. 143 is typically thought to represent 'I Love You' and that's true as well. Also, to be reassured that my angels are with me instills a level of confidence in me that I may have let drift. God dwells in me and I must be reminded of His presence as well during my human experience. We are enduring spiritual warfare and must be mindful of our influencers.

Angels or their darker form are guiding us either on a path of righteousness or one of destruction. The way to know who or what is guiding you, simply think and feel. Does it feel right? Do you think it is right? If both answers are yes, then proceed but continue to ask yourself these questions before decision making.

Also, synchronicities, a term coined by analytical psychologist Carl Jung, play a huge role in the guidance of life. Noticing numbers at specific times in life mean different things. This corresponds to Angel numbers too, which means that angels communicate with us through numbers. Seeing 11:11 means that doors are opened for you so be careful what you are asking for because you will most certainly receive it. Many see 11:11 and some even make a wish, be sure to utilize these opportunities to materialize your dreams. Also, be sure to assess your dreams to know if they are fixated on materials. Dream bigger than obtaining someone else's creation, we must be better than that. Dream to create!

Numbers are a universal language that we all need to consciously seek to understand. At the basis, we can study binary code which to my understanding is the actual universal language. Watching Ancient Aliens has me under the impression that even those that aren't from Earth are able to communicate through numbers, specifically 1's and 0's. There was a man on the show, who seen a UFO land and decided to go touch the ship, immediately after he experienced visions of 1's and 0's. He began to right down the entire code he saw and during the episode a portion was given to a gentleman who deciphered it.

Once we embrace our true nature, one of sheer curiosity we will be faced with an opportunity to discover Truth. Let's refer to the scene in the Matrix where Morpheus offers Neo the red and blue pill, this will be your experience. Red, you discover truth and you will never be the same again. Blue and you continue living the façade of your everyday life. Be true to yourself first and foremost if you expect to receive truth from the Universe.

Sea

Our first conversation, water
It was about water
Water brought us together
Water is forever
Another reason for Sea
Good things happen when you live faithfully

Both water signs
Pisces and Scorpio
I was ignoring the signs
That we should let it go
Going isn't always leaving
Just discover the reason
Sometimes it's more about the Leap n Reapin'
The blessing that was promised
The Harvest

Let us eat
With mastery of subtlety
Dancing, moving gracefully
Innerstanding artistry really is just a part of me
Even grasping concepts in Philosophy
You are a part of everything that I came to be
And thankfully
I pray for thee
To continue living prosperously

A.R.T

What is art? To me everything is art and I do mean every-thing. Of course, the typical aspects such as: drawing, painting, sculpting, etc. However, I have learned to include musical aspects as well, like: instrumentation, singing, dancing, etc. Also remember that fighting is an art form as well like boxing and martial arts.

Now, do you have to be fluent in these areas to be considered an artist? Yes, well in society's eyes you do, but you simply need to be fluent in a specific area. You can look at parenting as an art form, computer engineering, farming, and driving too. Anything where you are being your true Self is thought of as Art, because authenticity reveals truth.

Authenticity Reveals Truth is a universal law. Who you are is what you create but whether you know who you are is not for me to determine as I am still learning who I am. Be True to God and "His will will be done". The best outcome happens because it's for the *greater* good. Radiate Good energy into the life surrounding you and the cycle is repeated within said life.

Good is as Good does, Be Good and what you experience will be Good. Life is what you make it because we all live based on our choices/decisions. Everything you give is returned, typically with more energy when you factor in momentum. The truth you release will be presented back to you in the form of Truth. Authenticity is *being* as you are.

Acknowledge both the Natural *you* and the Spiritual *You* and intertwining them to experience God. Know more about who you truly are by Being who you truly are. Be confident that you are an exemplary being. This magnificent advice I am indeed giving to myself because I need this wisdom just as much as the next.

Coming from someone who didn't try much because I adopted the fear of failure during grade school.

I can remember teachers asking what we feared most and I never could think of much but hearing students answer failure, I agreed to answer the question and stay under the radar. Today, imagining I was playing it safer then, I must now spread my wings to experience the inner workings of the planet and the inner workings of life itself.

In my eyes, breathing is art; simply *being* will lead to Truth being revealed to you. I've learned that this is where the phrase "if you can breathe through it you can get through it" comes from. Remembering to breathe is a key that I must remember, I always have. Being authentic on even the most basic level is a display of discipline resulting in rewards that come in the form of knowledge.

The truth floods the mind and all you're left to do is apply through experience to receive wisdom. This condensed, concise lesson is what you pass on to the next individual, a summary if you will. Learn all there is to know and use this knowledge to explore this realm for truth followed by others.

Art is a way to authentically reveal truth because we are doing as we feel during creation; being yourself in a moment which becomes a masterpiece. If our creations can be masterpieces, what would that make the creator? Our Creator? ART transcends the Art we are exposed to and into all our Life experiences. Everything is Art because there's something more to all we encounter. Expand your consciousness to realize more as *you* are a being that exceeds even your most extreme expectations.

Yes, you can do everything you imagine and more, like my mom always told me "You can do anything you put your Mind to". This was the gem of all gems, only you should believe to know, although sometimes it is knowing then believing. But, as the Bible says, blessed are those who believe and have not seen. We can't physically see feelings deep within, but we are in our most creative state submerged with feelings.

My mom always said "you can do anything you put your mind to" whenever I'd ask if I was capable of something. What I was wanting to do then was minuscule, but the fact remained the same. A time for reflection is necessary. I'm learning today through remembering my foundation, how it has helped me immensely. Meditation is an art form that allows the Mind to freely experience reflection. They say focus on your breathing because it is the simple yet complex key to meditation. Inhale-exhale, simple, but you must maintain rhythm while experiencing meditation.

You will find yourself, initially, wanting to remain in the physical realm once you begin to travel. This comes in the form of your inability to remain quiet and still which is due to either not being taught the "how" or not wanting to deal with what awaits. It may be a bit of both which remains a part of the process of growth. Move on past the old you, the younger you, the immature you, to accept what was and learn how to *be*. Acknowledging the Past helps us to appreciate the Present, so we can create a better Future.

After "The Awakening", I began to see the world for what it is and Earth for who She is. Before the awakening I was unsure of a lot of things, myself, and God. At that time, I was going as those around me advised, slightly happy but still feeling what more was there for me to discover. Late December 2015, it hit me; The Bible was written by those that are like me, recording their Life experience. A powerful revelation indeed, my Faith in the authenticity had begun.

The next day, my car was repossessed while I was at the airport waiting on another pickup. This was my only source of income as well, imagine that, being out creating revenue and it comes to an end because you have no money. As soon as I think I am beginning to understand, this happens?! I had to request a ride through the same company to get home, the irony.

As I'm standing in the passenger pick up section at the Atlanta Domestic Terminal, all I could do was look up into the sky and say, "everything has to change?". Still in disbelief yet accepting the changes, I remained confused as to why the vehicle was repossessed for a mere week late payment.

I couldn't even fix myself to be angry because it was my responsibility to make the payments. I agreed to make them and failed to do so on the account of lacking discipline to perform a job that comes with no supervision.

Maybe the moment was premature, maybe it wasn't, maybe the lesson was to simply show me that I needed to develop discipline in order to be successful at anything and everything.

Driving is synonymous with Life and be sure to remember that both are a dear privilege. To me, it's all about how smooth you wish the ride to be and the best drivers are ones who do not disturb their occupants, including themselves. While riding on a multilane street or highway, this will be your best test to see what you've got. Keep the vehicle moving at a constant, steady, imperative pace and know you have the option to switch lanes when other drivers are impeding your progress.

If you are approaching a red light release your foot from the accelerator, meaning if you know the decision you are thinking of making is hasty think carefully over it. Use your blinkers, be courteous always, mind your manners and do not be a hypocrite; one cannot complain about people who are rude if one has road rage. Neither one of you have control over your emotions making you more alike than you tend to realize. If we had more discipline, we would be able to better manage any situation we encounter.

Many of my greatest epiphanies come during the storms I am to weather. The down times make me remember to look up, also sending me back into a space of seeking more knowledge. Knowledge from those that have weathered the storms to know it's not what you perceive, nonetheless everything you perceive. The storm is a figment of your imagination, yet it remains oh so real.

"Fear is a choice, danger is real", a quote that comes from Will Smith in After Earth. The darkness I endure strengthens the Light I carry. Being engulfed in darkness knowing you are the Light only makes your shine stronger and brighter, conditioning you for the journey ahead. Everything encountered is to prepare you for what lies ahead. Thinking of circumstances as preparation will make the situations bearable.

Even during one of my very few intimate relationships, I was experiencing the darker days of my life. I remember being in a state of depression for like two to three days, simply not happy. I wasn't feeling it every day I woke up and I would sit in front of the computer moping but rather numb. Although she was my light, my escape from my reality I was still forced to endure when I was alone. I didn't like to be alone, but I didn't want to be around anyone either. I felt like a failure because I didn't feel I was making any progress like my peers who were away at college.

Instead I was always at home because I mismanaged any money I collected. My creativity was at an all-time low as I was only into materials and my better half was unimpressed to say the least. Inviting her to come over just to sit in another house and waste a day away watching programs I had no desire to watch. I needed her energy to keep me afloat and it did, thank you Sea.

Understanding the very basics of life today, I have narrowed it down to its simplest concept. I can do what I want, and I will prevail with faith. Faith in God, Self and Life is where it starts. Life is energy which only transforms. The body is the last stage of development because it is mostly controlled by the Mind and Spirit. If done sequentially, enhancing the Spirit and Mind leads to everything in the Body to being corrected. It takes a little to control a lot.

Feel the power you possess because you create your reality. The realm we typically witness is the result of our consciousness which is influenced by energy. Realize that until the spirit is renewed and cleansed, your mind is susceptible to disorder. A cleansed strong Spirit has the power to change any situation. The mind and spirit combined focused on fruition is even more powerful, many call this intent. Thoughts become reality so guard your thoughts and your feelings. Separate you from You, Self from the mind. Allow them to blend but be able to detach them from one another. When the spirit and mind are on the same track, the body naturally follows suit.

The body communicates in feeling, different from those of the mind but still connected. The body either feels good or is in pain, and pain is a symbol for growth. Nurture the source of the pain after innerstanding the location. Nurturing helps to alleviate all the side effects, allowing the body to grow. Naturally when we feel pain, we massage where we feel the discomfort. Do not take this instinct lightly, we are natural healers. As we unite our spirit, mind and body realize how to heal any and every ailment you possess but also remember to only claim health to be healthy. Work to innerstand the vessel you walk in to better innerstand your next move towards the *cure*.

The body goes where the eyes lead meaning accuracy is initially dependent upon sight. If your sight is good your aim will be too. Imagine shooting a paper ball into a trashcan. The more you focus on where you want the ball to go the higher your chances of making the shot. Focusing on the result so heavily that your body naturally computes the algorithms on the specifics of force, arc, and release to make the shot. This is also the case in the sport basketball. Only difference being in the sport, athletes have reached the muscle memory phase meaning the body remembers the specifics needed for success.

If the body recollects memory, then the other aspects of you can put focus elsewhere. At least theoretically, it would be most efficient sometimes to put all your focus on one task such that it is completed as efficiently as possible. Other times it would be best for you to indulge in multitasking, so you can learn more at once.

I made my own regimen and it's really become my very own practice. Part yoga due to the poses and stretches but continuously in motion so it's dance-like. Rhythmic naturally, it provides for a strengthened spine. Simply moving is "exercise" to the body, the main thing is activity, be active. You can straighten your spine if you move the right way in more than one way. Then the muscles need to be even, so get an even distribution. Also remember that you can massage the pain away.

You don't have to live in pain, but we must all live with pain as pain is a natural experience we must learn to endure. Feel the energy pulsate through your palms and soles and utilize this energy within to restore balance.

Remember to breathe as breathing expands the lungs, stretching the lungs and the rib cage. Energy is released in burps, farts, and pops.

My energy is transformed as I dance, dancing is rhythmic yoga, so it is a healing art form. Fighting is like dancing that's why it used to be said "let's dance". It was seen as such but in a different form and a bit more physical. Only professional fighters see their sport as art today and those that are heavily into it. I am neither, I have simply accepted my decision to be the one who comprehends.

Dancing allows me to feel my energy flow intensely, with every movement I can shift energy to the correct place. With every pop, burp or fart I know energy is moving and needs to transform or be released into the atmosphere to be re-received in another area. It happens simultaneously but that is what happens when I allow my body to move freely while maintaining a rhythm.

We must start again from One to really understand again what's what and why it is what it is. Since no one explains Life, which I feel is necessary if we are to live better, one must need to know more about Life, real life. As the Mind expands we need to revisit what we once dreamt to understand and grasp these concepts.

For me relearning is fun, but my focus is heavily rooted in new knowledge that I lose track of relationships. I must remember to nurture my relationships rather than being solely focused on learning something new although it's inspiring. Life is in concepts or moments; each moment is a moment on its own but also part of One continuous moment we can all learn from.

To live is to learn so learn to live, efficiency is a key that needs to be recognized. Grasp this key and use it to unlock the many doors that are ahead. Learning what it means to live comes first then you can apply Life lessons everywhere in Life. Life lessons transcend into all areas of Life, your life to be more specific. These transcendent lessons imply just how well you are beginning to innerstand Life. To understand Life means you put Life above you or as something to be attained but to innerstand means you accept what is and travel deeper to reach realizations within. Revelations come in waves when you tune in and acknowledge the present moment as simply what is.

Many of our original tongues are read form right to left, uniting the feeling realm with the thinking realm. In the western hemisphere, the left side of the brain or thought is the focal point in education with neglect to intuition. This is purposeful to weaken you such that you will be easily dominated in the realm you are taught to neglect. This creates a disconnect from the Spiritual energy you have access to. The original tongues are authentic and thus reveal truth; from feminine came the life of man but from masculine came the feminine creation.

Even though this is true, remember the saying, 'it's darkest before light", think in terms of Yin and Yang but only in authenticity is Truth revealed. That's why we must read books such as the Bible and Quran while living what is said. Feel for the message and live your life being true to you because only when you are true to You will your life align, and you see Truth.

Trees

Trees
Come from seeds
Feed your needs
But are sadly
Under a travesty
All for money
What a scam
You think you're being beneficial
And bam!
It hit you
Whatever "they" want you to do
Is not what's best for Y O U

Why

The reason behind
Is the reason to try
At least in my mind
No why is like being left dry
Why
Because you said so
Well I said no
So who is in the right
Follow the one on the right
As I do, especially when I write
About doing what's right
Even in the night
I continue to shine bright
Because I AM Light

Truth

Truth is, history is biased and the term itself lets you know; look around to see if *life* is how you were taught. I know personally, learning of past events through an unfiltered lens can be infuriating. Many of us feel like we are educated because we have a certification stating we've completed the prerequisites but we're just as ignorant as the people that failed to complete. It's a tough pill to swallow when you learn of the atrocities melanated people of all shades endured so that you can live today.

Learning of the Truth instills humility and a sense of pride knowing the blood you share is with warriors. We come from a long line of elite warriors that not only excelled in the art of fighting but the mastery of education. Our ancestors were brilliant scholars, proficient in everything from astrology, to biochemistry, down to construction, to mathematics, etc. They tell us we began as slaves, but we have a rich past that would be best received if discovered through your own research.

When you uncover Truth, your present moment makes more sense allowing you to move past everything and invest energy into yourself. It's us realizing we do not need much, at least in the physical world, but we need to look within and work from the inside out. Even in sports the same concept exists. Take basketball, many coaches prefer to play inside-out, meaning score closer to the basket before shooting from further away. Giving yourself the opportunity to gain momentum leading to easier scoring. In football, many coaches prefer to run the ball before engaging in the pass.

My generation has the stereotype of "procrastinators/lazy". Truth is we are bored with the life we feel we are forced to live. We make a game out of life by doing things at the "last minute" because it's a strategy. We call it being "clutch", which is a skill many people have a fun time experiencing. We must enjoy life on some scale and we get a rush out of getting work done in a timely fashion to make the challenge more intense. We love to be challenged, thus we put ourselves in tougher situations than necessary for the thrill. We must innerstand that we can have this same level of excitement simply walking the path given. Make the right decision when compelled to, utilize the conscience. We always have a choice. Always. Children may have less of a choice because they typically have more to learn about life's necessities.

Now adults on the other hand, make every decision to lead them to their status. You may feel you don't have options, but you always have at least two options. You always have a for or against choice. 'For' does not correspond to 'Yes' either, it is not a guarantee that everything you are in favor of is what you need to do. Only make decisions when you should, that's what my generation has realized. That's why we wait until we must make a move to make a move. We must know it's for real before we take action.

We must consistently, rather than sporadically look back at history to teach us what to do next or what to do now because the present moment determines the future and the past. All I want to do is inspire others to search for the truth as I did. Do not simply take my words as truth because it aligns to make sense. Do your own research to discover what is true and why it is true. Only at this juncture will you truly understand and realize that it all makes sense now. Simply taking another's word as truth is what our issue, as a whole, is. Think for yourself and do for yourself if you ever wish to be free.

People just want to feel important, they want to feel valued. They want a sense of purpose, naturally. Encoded in our DNA is our purpose, we feel purpose but now we must discover what it looks like in the material realm.

Feeling and Thoughts translating into reality usually don't appear to be what they seem. When turning dreams into reality, you must be able to recognize when you are winning. That's where humility comes in as well. You don't have to continue too long and search for more.

Learn how to utilize that which you have already acquired and create. Creating is our purpose as Humans or God-bodies. And our creations must be beneficial to mankind or we don't feel like we have fulfilled our purpose. There's a reason for that, we haven't. If a human doesn't create or their creation isn't beneficial to life we have work to do still.

Now we must explore the other attributes we possess. The system is designed to make the products feel connected to the producer. The product is made to believe that their only chance of better comes from the producer. So, they exhaust energy into the producer, trusting that products would be better. They may seemingly get better but it's only the producers keeping all gains and doing it all over again with different products. We make every decision for ourselves. Really begin to make decisions according to what is best for you. But before you can begin to fathom what's best for you let alone what's good for you, you must understand You.

Begin to seek knowledge about your origins and life's origins. You'll begin to gradually understand more and more of the simple complexities of life. Your mind will begin opening to receive. As of now many are only open to receive that which they've *been* seeing because it constantly calls for more. They don't get a chance to process anything real, they won't understand what real is.

If they don't understand real, they don't understand what they need because they are real indulging in fiction. Reality television, News, and Fast food are fiction, meaning they don't offer much substance, if any, but they may leave you feeling satisfied momentarily.

They don't tell you the truth and after learning of a little, I can see why, because it's all fabrication to make themselves seem humane. They told you about Hitler, exaggerated it, but kept Leopold a secret. The main difference between them is the skin pigmentation of the individuals killed. Hitler went after Jew-ish peoples while Leopold went to the heart of Africa in Congo to decimate their culture. In search of black gold, rubber to fuel the booming vehicle age, Leopold killed upwards to ten million Africans during the late 1800s, early 1900s.

The moment you realize you remain hungry for knowledge, is the moment they are showing you what's "new". None of it is new it's just rereleased in a different order. The moment someone feeds you a little real for the first time in a long time, you will yearn for more. For the first time, you will finally feel substance. Substance is very fulfilling, and it takes less to lead to contentment.

If your appetite is contained, you can divert energy towards creation. After consumption, we can focus again. Although sometimes after consumption we have exhausted so much energy in obtaining that we sleep soon after. After consumption and rest, the only thing left for us to do is work. As far as the body is concerned, feed it, rest it, work it. Our genuine work is creation. We are creators as God is the Creator.

Now that you innerstand you are a creator also, the question I love to ask comes next, *why*? If you don't know the "why", why do it? As a kid growing up, if I didn't know the reasoning for doing something, I did it on my own time regardless of the consequences. Typically, it'd just have to be my mother repeating what she told me to do, which annoyed me just as much as it frustrated her, but I wasn't speeding up my process unless I wanted to.

Because I wasn't receiving many explanations, the lack of answers made me find a reason to do as I was told. I had to become more annoyed than curious to learn why I am to do as I am told. I understand the purpose of doing what your parents say but the simple, tedious tasks were another story. This included cleaning my room, the kitchen, bathroom, and anything that had to do with cleaning. I didn't fully understand why this level of tidiness was the standard, so I had to be told on numerous occasions, several times to do something minute.

All I ever wanted was an answer to my "why". I asked why several times, but it was always met as if why was a challenge, maybe it was my tone or maybe it's the word itself, but my why's are out of curiosity and eagerness to learn how more is connected. I wanted to be able to explain to someone else the meaning behind actions versus simply doing as I was told.

Still a good kid, I did do some reckless things to show just how key at least answering a why, is. I remember running my mother's phone bill up to a thousand dollars because I asked to get unlimited texting which was about twenty dollars extra and was met with a no. The no was normal, I had gotten used to no being the first thing I was told, but when the why is always "because I said so", don't expect me to comply.

Now, I have learned over the years that you don't use extra resources when you don't have to. Seems simple enough today to tell a thirteen-year-old that. Now, I'm almost certain that would've turned into a healthy dialogue to reach the bottom line instilling wisdom even younger. At the time, I'm not sure if she had the words to explain or was another "too tired" to engage.

Which leads me to another issue I have with our current system. They separate the home by removing the provider, the father, and pulling away the nurturer, the mother. Many fathers are wrongly persecuted or supremely distracted. And by the time the mothers make it back home, they are all nurtured out because they've used their gift elsewhere to provide. Pulling away women from the homes was engineered to create a dysfunctional generation.

By the grace of God, I had men in my life to teach me by example the way of a Man. My father, Uncle, Step-Father, and older Brother are my guides to manhood. They are my emotional, physical, spiritual, and mental masters. They may not know their impact on me but hoped to have one and now they know just how impactful they have been in my life.

I was captivated by my older brother's perspective, always wanting to be nearby to listen to what he had to say. Everything was new to me; some things are still new to me, but I was naïve then. No one could tell me anything but him. He was one of the few I felt understood me so talking to anyone else just wasn't the same. He always spoke with such compassion that I knew anytime he gave advice it was in my best interest. I say advice because that's how it felt when I was told to do something, I was given a choice. He would never force his hand because it's not his role to do so and he always left me with a decision to make.

Now more than ever I appreciate all, ALL that he taught me. Much of which he wouldn't even know came from him, but it did nonetheless. Many always wonder why I am the way I am, I'd give him a lot of the credit. My greatest influence, my biggest role model growing up. I would even try to imitate but soon found out our paths are not the same. I was supposed to understand what a role model was, then all I did was observe. Observing many of his moves, occasionally asking the results and learning from his mistakes, I learned all I could while I could, answering all the why's I was able to think of. I was a sponge absorbing all that I could from him. It went from me trying to be him to me being an evolution of him.

As I evolve, I can only imagine how simple the life of a human was when Adam and Eve were living; take a trip with me. First off, they were the only two, no clothing, no jobs. Although they didn't have jobs they did have to work to live. They grew their own food in the Garden of Eden. As humans during this time we only knew what was right.

It wasn't until Adam ate from the Tree of Knowledge that Man was able to see the full scope as God could. Man being very immature, hid from God because they realized they weren't clothed. Now they can experience shame and fear while before Adam ate the apple all we knew was Love. Man knew nothing but Love for creation.

Then we get to our more advanced cultures and I can't help but wonder what were the pyramids for? A question few have been able to answer, but from my understanding they are beacons which harness Gaia energy within earth. Gaia is a limitless reservoir, if you will, of pure energy which can be used as a power source. The significance of the triangle being the most basic strongest shape is to be noted as well. In vortex math, the triangle aligns with three, six, and nine and this is no *coincidence* as those are simply an occurrence we have not determined the meaning behind.

Pyramids are all over the Earth, including in Antarctica! And they all are resurrected on Ley Lines or the higher energy locations of our *home*. I'm thinking ancient cultures utilized these lines as a means of communication and exploration. I'll find myself traveling to see pyramids up close and in person to discover truth for myself one day.

The Ankh, an ancient symbol, much older than the cross, is a symbol for the human body as well as many other natural phenomena. The loop representing the head followed by the arms stretched out to feel the whole body. As you stand erected, arms outstretched, while extending your neck to be as tall as possible one is healing the skeletal system. Everything on you can be felt if you maintain concentration. See and Feel with your Third Eye as you heal your body to be good.

Ankh means Life and to carry an ankh is to carry the Key to Life. We are the Key to Life, humans, God. Since we are made in His/Her image we are as God is, we have that potential. Life is about evolution and humans are to evolve. God is Life so the Key to Life is God. One big circle to confirm everything is everything, only difference being the language. Biblically there was once one world language and following the Tower of Babel, the language was scrambled.

Today we reference a one world government yet again. We do not need to speak the same language to communicate with one another. We are intelligent being capable of learning more than one form of communication. We must see that we are not to simplify our lives by inefficient living. Live like wolves and govern ourselves. Allow different tribes to be and work together in unison towards a common goal of evolution. Learn what you are capable of. As humans, we can do so much more than we realize. The Bible says we are to do greater works than Jesus. I don't know about you, but I want to know what all that intel's. If Jesus can resurrect the dead and then himself, I want to know what's next after that.

Be a Healthy Being

There's something everywhere you go
But the something you pay attention to
Changes as you grow
As it is true, time will tell
This is key, all will always be well

Continue until you no longer grow but evolve
And soon you will see the issue dissolve
Conflicts resolve
And all because you never stalled

Mastery of Self is the goal
One of the greatest illusions, getting ol'
Because time is relative
And even as the lessons become repetitive
We must remember to continuously give

Give anything
Give everything
I mean
It is only a thing
A thing you cannot bring
Into the Heaven-xing

L's

Accept the things you cannot change, change the things you can change but have the wisdom to know the difference.

My uncle told me this on Mother's Day in 2015, a major lesson I needed time to reflect on and grow with. In life, there are times where what we experience is something that is out of our control but influences us. The passing of a loved one would be a great example of an occurrence that you don't have control over. In this instance, we must accept the circumstances to keep our Spirits strong through Faith and persevere. Anything that we can live to accept we must have the ability to change it. Truly assess a situation you experience to determine whether you can make a direct difference. Develop the ability to self evaluate and adjust accordingly.

If you can't change the people around you, change the people around you

This lesson coming from one of my school mom's, Ms. Silveri, a gem that I have continuously said to myself throughout life. The individuals you surround yourself with will determine how far in life you go. As we grow, we want to continue to grow because of all we are now capable of. As we continue to grow, everyone will not share our sentiments when it comes to growth. If one isn't constantly growing, then stagnation may seep into our lives. We cannot allow anything other than growth to unfold in our lives, so some of your peers, friends, and even family will have to be left behind if they don't maintain your pace. We cannot force people to change with us but we can let them know through our actions that we will not let them prevent us from changing.

Move On

We must be able to move on from any situation. No matter what we go through, we can take a moment to reflect and accept, but keep it moving. Growth is a continuous process and we honestly cannot afford for anything to impede our progress. In a sense, we must take what we experience by the wayside while we experience more as we learn more. Moving on can be one of the harder things to do because we all have a genuine desire to help others but when we have exhausted our resources we must continue without them. I would speak on moving on from materials but at this point we shouldn't be attached to anything we have the power to create as we can create better. It's the moving on from experiences that can be tough, like: graduating, moving out, moving to another state, changing your relationship status, etc. The constant battle of should I stay, or should I go, in these moments confess your truth and follow your intuition.

Take your L

Accountability is a major key in life. Along with Patience, Balance and Love, Accountability is just as important for humankind. Accountability is having the conscious ability to recognize what's the true cause to an effect. Develop the capability to distinguish when you are at fault. L doesn't have to mean loss as we'd typically see it expressed. L can also mean lesson, learn to receive your lesson. Be teachable, always willing to learn more and expound on the knowledge you currently have. Lessons are what prepare you for what's to come, your future, which are based on what happened, your past. Learning the lesson as it is given puts you in position to Ace the tests that are inevitably on the way.

Stay ready

The only thing you can be certain of is that change is coming, again. Change is the only constant in our ever-shifting lives. Things can change at a moment's notice or over the course of years. Either way we must be prepared for that which we know is coming. Become soft as water to remain mutable to any of the adjusting currents. Staying ready is about learning on the fly and retaining composure to complete the assigned tasks. Stay ready for the eminent change that is upon us because you never know when you'll need to apply those lessons. Tomorrow is not promised but today is as we are living today every day. Always be sure that you are in constant preparation for that which you asked for, typically success.

You can do anything you put your Mind to

My mother told me this all while I was growing up and I'm only just beginning to understand the magnitude of this lesson as a young adult. The mind is our most powerful, most useful, most feared gift we have as humans. Our mind is the only thing no one can control, ever, no matter what anyone says. Only you have the power to control or relinquish control over your mind. Maintaining the driver seat of your mind may seem easy but to those who know, it is an extremely difficult as you'll first have to overcome your fears. Overcoming your fears starts as recognition and after you've recognized the issue you solve it. Now it's time to see what you can create using your gift from God.

Live in the Present

Lao Tzu says, "if you experience depression, you're living in the past; if you experience anxiety, you're living in the future; and you are at peace when you live in the present". This also a lesson in After Earth when Will Smith's character urges his son to root himself in the present moment to live beyond fear. Living in the present keeps you conscious of the fact that you are good, this keeps you in a state of bliss creating a reality filled with joy and love. Living in the present is about only concerning yourself with what you can do better to have improved results.

Expand your Consciousness

To evolve into greater beings, we must grow where we need growth the most, our minds. If we can get our minds to encompass more, to receive more, we will be able to do more. Not solely gaining new abilities but improved efficiency in understanding complexities. The more we expand our consciousness, the more perspective we have on everything experienced. Much of our daily lives are lived on autopilot and this is not the way to live. We are to know what we are doing while we are doing it and it should be the right thing to do. Expansion is a fun process as you begin to see much more, however you must remember to remain responsible. Also, with expansion, realms begin to unite to become *one*, the ultimate goal.

Keep going

Be sure to always keep moving, although you feel fatigued you must continue moving forward. If you can't physically move then move mentally, see yourself continuing the journey in your mind. You may be pleasantly surprised at how much further you can go when you use your mind accordingly. Since you are consistently progressing, you must have foresight as well. Foresight is recognizing any dangers up ahead and adjusting the course to keep safe. Foresight is a skill few have and those without find themselves in avoidable mishaps.

Remember to look up

I am receiving new revelation on this phrase daily at this point. At first, I was taking it in the literal sense, still accurate, as looking up elongates the spine and opens the chest when you roll the shoulders back. Then I went spiritual, looking up to God, to remembering where I came from, the stars. I look at the sky regularly, admiring the clouds and the depth of my visuals. And just recently, I added on remembering to look up from working so much. Remember that although the projects will help the people, you too help the people by remaining inclusive to their lives. I have the tendency to isolate when I go into a state of working to sustain concentration which comes off as alienation to my loved ones. It makes them feel like I don't want to be around them for whatever reason, then whenever the projects are complete people may not resonate because you didn't nurture relationships.

Locate the pain and heal it at the Source

See when we feel any physical pain, we have the power to heal. Literally we can see in our mind where the pain is located and visualize it dissolving as we direct energy toward the area needing healing. This was essential in my healing from scoliosis and the misconfiguration left behind. I was to endure the pain first then see where I felt discomfort and ease it away. Whether we massage physical pain, or we maneuver through mental pain, we should find where it begins to truly heal the ailment. This is not an enjoyable process, at least not to me, because addressing the most tender areas of our lives can be challenging. All great challenges though, lead to our greatest triumphs. Going into those darker, unchartered waters of my mind, I was to maintain the drive to complete the task, healing. And I want to thank myself for continuing to heal every day. Thank you, Khadeem Jibreel Thomas.